A Woman's Guide
to Manifestation

A Woman's Guide to Manifestation

CREATING YOUR REALITY WITH CONSCIOUS INTENT

BIANCA GUERRA

LIVING LIFE PUBLISHING CO.

San Antonio, Texas
Sausalito, California

You may order directly from the publisher.

For information about permission to
reproduce excerpts from this book write to:

Living Life Publishing Co.
24165 IH-10 West, Suite 217-474
San Antonio, Texas 78257
Office: 210-698-6392 • Fax: 210-698-6394
OR
1001 Bridgeway Blvd. #704
Sausalito, California 94965
Office: 415-331-9222 • Fax: 415-332-8422
OR
E-mail: LivingLifePublishing@msn.com
www.LivingLifePublishing.com

Library of Congress Control Number
2005926301
ISBN 0-9768773-1-7
Printed in China by Palace Press International
First Edition

The publisher commissioned Garret Moore to create the cover image entitled
Manifestation.

All other images are copyright © Digital Vision/Getty Images Pictures, Brand
X/Getty Images Pictures, Photodisc/Getty Images Pictures, or Comstock/Getty
Images Pictures.

Graphic Designer: Diane Rigoli

Editor: Judy Gitenstein

Editorial Consultants: Lou CasaBianca, Susan Grodnick and Cynthia Rubin

Dedication

*L*earning to become a feminine, receptive and loving individual has been a lifelong journey for me. I want to dedicate this book to all the people who have entered my life contributing to my understanding and experience of what is, and isn't, an openhearted, receptive, loving, and nurturing woman. I especially want to thank my two sons, Edwin and Ryan Hockaday, who, by the very nature of their birth, helped open my heart to love at a level I had not before experienced. They have been my teachers, my mirrors and my guides. I love them dearly and thank them for allowing me to walk down this path of motherhood and Divine co-creation.

I also want to acknowledge and thank my only sister, Sylvia Meckel, who has been my friend, confidante and support throughout my entire life. If there is a definition of sisterly love, it is my sister at my side, and on my side, loving, counseling and accepting me just as I am. She has shown me, through example, the many faces of the feminine, receptive woman. I love her for loving me unconditionally and for teaching me how to be accepting without judgment.

Finally, I want to thank my soul mate and fiancé, Lou CasaBianca, without whose love and support I would not have written this book. He has helped me create a safe and loving environment that lends itself to manifesting my heart's desires. He supports and encourages my journey of self-discovery into the realm of limitless possibilities. He is my partner, my teacher and my love. To him I give my heartfelt appreciation for choosing to travel this journey with me of helping to awaken my inner feminine and my Divine loving goddess.

Table of Contents

Preface

As a single mother of two young men, a businesswoman, founder of a physical therapy and sports medicine clinic, medical intuitive, philanthropist, and teacher at heart, I've experienced much in the arena of health and healing and have discovered that not everything is as it appears. There are many faces to illness and many modes of healing. From working with my patients, my friends and family, and through my own experiences, I've learned that remarkable results and recovery from disease and illness can occur following a change in a person's mindset. I have discovered that once people become conscious and understand to some degree why they became ill, they are usually on the road to recovery.

I have realized that there are certain steps that must be taken to manifest health and wellness. I had begun, somewhat unconsciously at first, to apply these concepts to different areas within my life—relationships, career, and finances—and realized that the same formula was used in each scenario. It wasn't until I was asked by a dear friend to teach her how I was manifesting within my life that I sat down and began to analyze seriously what it was I was doing that brought the results I wanted. It was a challenge, yet I accepted it. I truly wanted to help my friend bring wonderful things into her life.

I would like to help you bring wonderful things into your life, too. In this book I offer you my experiences with the hope they will help you to understand and develop the personal power of manifestation within your life. I wrote it for those of you who know there is something out there that you haven't tapped into yet. I hope it will give you the tools to gather the wisdom and knowledge to create your own world of beauty, light, and love— a world unaffected by worry, fear, or doubt.

When this world of light and love is used for your betterment, magnificent and noble manifestations will result. I rejoice in your beauty and support your journey into the realm of manifestation within your life.

Bianca Guerra
Sausalito, California; San Antonio, Texas
January 2005

Chapter One

The Eight Steps to Manifestation:

Tuning in, Creating Your Goals and Heart's Desires

Find Your
Purpose in Life

– One –

The Eight Steps to Manifestation:
Tuning in, Creating Your Goals and Heart's Desires

*W*hat does manifestation mean to you? To me it represents the creating of something from nothing, the bringing forth of a goal or desire.

It has been proven that you can manifest what you focus on, either consciously or unconsciously. If you focus on loving others, you in turn will attract loving people and positive situations. If you are angry and impatient—when driving, for example—you might attract other drivers who demonstrate signs of road rage. If you are enthusiastic about a project, your enthusiasm can inspire others to join you. If you are joyful and laugh often with abandon, you can attract others who will join in the laughter.

Laughter is contagious—most emotions are. Have you ever found yourself crying when a friend or loved one experienced an emotional or physical pain? It's as if you were sharing the pain. I was once playing at a friend's house during grade school when her mother became ill and began vomiting. My friend almost instantly began gagging and heaving as if she wanted to vomit. She was sharing her mother's pain.

You probably are aware that the more deeply you focus on a task, the purer your intention becomes, and the greater the results can be. The more you want something, the harder you will work toward achieving it, and the likelier you will be to acquire it.

There is a key element in the realization of your dreams, goals, and desires and that is to know what it is you REALLY want to manifest or create. Too often, confusion and disappointment will creep into your life if you are giving yourself, others, God, and the Universe mixed messages about what you want.

Let's say you decide that you want to become a better person who chooses to take the high road in disagreements. You've decided that you will steer clear of shouting matches. You promise yourself that if you get into a disagreement with someone, you will remain calm, stay centered, and stand your ground while keeping your heart open to love and understanding. You've convinced yourself you truly want to create communication without shouting and turmoil. Then you come across someone you know who doesn't share your beliefs. You strongly feel that if you were to bring up certain topics in that person's presence the chances are high that there would be a disagreement that might lead to shouting. You ask yourself, "Should I bring that up?" Your final decision is to broach the delicate yet volatile topic.

Although your conscious mind may want to mature and evolve beyond a shouting match, the possibility still exists that your baser instinct will invite turmoil. Look closely at yourself and your life to see what it is you really want and then look at what it is you might be creating or manifesting. You might discover that you are sending yourself and others mixed messages.

Suppose you want to quit smoking and decide to join a self-help group that tries the "one day at a time" approach. You seem to be doing well and are feeling okay, yet you find yourself going to a cocktail bar where people are smoking and seemingly having a wonderful time. You inhale the swirling smoke, which prompts you to want a cigarette. You are giving yourself and the Universe mixed messages about your intention to quit smoking. If you feel you really and truly want to quit, then you need to look more deeply at why you enjoy hanging around people who smoke.

Try to take the time to tune into yourself and follow the guidelines from your Higher Self, your God-self. Open your heart to listen and begin implementing the wisdom from within you to reach your goals and manifest your heart's desires. Trust the guidance you are given from your inner Divinity. This will be one of the best barometers you will have, learn to follow your instincts and your hunches.

Your external support teams—your family, friends, co-workers, teachers, and others—are important, to some degree, in helping to give you feedback, yet the ultimate and most trustworthy sounding board is your inner guidance. You will find that the people in your life often reflect back to you what you already know. This makes for great confirmation, yet isn't really necessary if you are tuning into your inner guidance. Once you've established a relationship with your inner guidance, and once you begin to trust the process, you will have little doubt as to the direction to take in any situation.

How do you know whether you are getting inner guidance from your Divine self or from your analytical mind? Here are some clues: When your Divine self is communicating with you, you might feel a strong sense of peacefulness and calm, a feeling that all will be well. You might also get a strong idea of what needs to be done. Sometimes there is little logic in your message, yet that sense of peacefulness is always present. There is no doubt, no second-guessing, just a deep inner knowing of what to do.

Conversely, when you are not tuning into your inner Divinity, but are trying to get answers from your analytical mind, you generally toss answers back and forth and envision many possible scenarios. You might feel uncertain of your answers, so you seek advice outside yourself from just about everyone close to you, and sometimes from those who are not, trying to find THE answer to your problem or situation. Watch and examine yourself during those moments of searching for answers.

The more you follow through and act on the guidance given to you from your inner Divinity, the more you will experience the full, joyful aspect of life. The more you learn to trust your inner guidance and instinct, the more you will manifest what you truly want.

The Eight Steps to Manifestation

*I*n analyzing how I manifest in my life, I have discovered that there are eight clear steps that I follow—in order—every time I manifest something. I will outline them here and cover them in more detail throughout the book.

1. DESIRE. All creation begins with a desire for something. The more energy infused into the desire and the more your heart is involved in this process, the stronger the force will be to assist you with your manifestation. So, begin with a heartfelt emotion, a burning desire.

2. THOUGHT. Desire is then transferred into the mental body, where you begin thinking of ways to create/manifest what you want. The more you focus on how you are to manifest your desire, the likelier you will be to create it. If you can visualize what you want to manifest and can see yourself getting it, this will add power to your manifestation. Focusing your thoughts and images like a laser beam is a strong and powerful tool to assist with your manifestation.

3. VERBAL PROCLAMATION. Speaking your thoughts and desires out loud begins setting the manifestation in motion. You can either state what it is you want or ask God and the Universe to assist you in manifesting what you want. In speaking out loud, you are demonstrating to the Universe, to the world, to your friends and family that you are going to manifest your desires. The more you speak the words with conviction, as if what they describe has already occurred, the likelier it will be that they will manifest.

4. BELIEF. Knowing 100 percent, like an innocent child, that you will succeed in creating your heart's desires is essential for your manifestation. Believe, without question or doubt, that you will create and manifest what it is you've proclaimed to God and the Universe. Believe that you deserve the results of your creation.

5. RECEIVING. Receiving is an integral part of the process of manifesting. Open your heart and drop into your feminine/receptive mode, and allow yourself to receive the wonderful gifts of your creation. By being in your feminine/receptive mode, you allow yourself to receive the object of your desires. By "feminine/receptive," I'm not implying you have to be a female to manifest, only that you must embody this feminine quality of receptivity.

6. GROUNDING INTO THE PHYSICAL. Once you receive the object of your desires, you can then integrate it and ground it into the feminine earth for its physical manifestation. By grounding, I mean that you take the energy of your desire, claim it as yours, and allow the physical form to take shape. The more you connect with Mother Earth and her feminine principles of creation and birth, the likelier you will be to manifest your desires.

7. LETTING GO. Allowing God and the Universe to take over and orchestrate the how, when, where, and why of your creation is vital to its manifestation. The harder you struggle for control over universal law, the more difficult it will be to manifest your desires. You've done your part by setting the intent. Allow God and the Universe to determine the particulars. Allow the process to occur in Divine time. If you do so, you will find that the results of your manifestation are far greater and more beautiful than what you had originally imagined.

8. GRATITUDE. Giving thanks to God, the Universal Intelligence, is one of the steps that help to self-perpetuate manifestation. By acknowledging that you have received help from some other level that you have tapped into—Divinity—you are stating that it is done. It is like saying "Amen." You are giving finality to your manifestation and setting up the cycle for more manifestation down the road.

The chapters that follow will help you discover and clarify your life's purpose and understand the role of your feminine quality in manifestation. They will outline the areas where manifestation can be utilized and give you a clear understanding of the difference between manifestation and manipulation. They will go into depth on the stumbling blocks that keep you from manifesting your heart's desires.

Follow the eight steps to manifestation and you will open the doors to another way of living, one in which you are the commander and co-creator of your world and what's in it. Be willing to look at life a little differently and to see all the possibilities your life can offer you. Paint your own picture of life that you can share with others!

Surrender to the Higher Intelligence within you and marvel at the beauty you can create in your life. Learn to become your own best friend and enjoy the confidence that results from it. Manifest your goals, your heart's desires, and become one with your Divinity.

Blessings to you on this journey through life and may the tools of manifestation benefit you and others.

Let us begin.

Chapter Two

Knowing What You Want from Life

Decide What You
Want to Create

– Two –

Knowing What You Want from Life

*T*he idea to create or change something comes from a desire to do so. This is the first step to manifestation. A desire for a gold medal in the Olympics drives an athlete to more intense and productive practices and stimulates that person to keep the body in tip-top shape. The reward for such hard work is receiving the gold medal.

How do you know if what you think you want is REALLY what you want and need? How can you determine the difference between the two?

These two questions are not as easy to answer as you might think. You may have plenty of ideas of what you want. You may want to make more money or to get your body into better shape or to be more loving to yourself and others. Perhaps you want a better job or to move into a larger and more beautiful home or want to have more joy and happiness for yourself and your family. The list could go on and on.

You may generally do things or want things because somewhere down the line there is a reward for you. So, if you were to understand what it is that drives you to want to create or change something in your life and fully understand the rewards you will be getting, then you can most certainly be creating what it is you TRULY want. By this I mean that if you were more conscious of what is driving you to want something, then you can be more in control of what it is that you do to achieve it.

What is it that drives a bulimic, for example, to binge-eat and then purge? Do you think that the bulimic really is that hungry or really wants to vomit? I don't think so! Let me tell you from my experience. Yes, you do get the urge to eat and, on some level, it's a frantic urge that propels you into the kitchen to begin looking for food. You look through the refrigerator, the cabinets, and the pantry for ANYTHING to eat that will help you satisfy this insatiable hunger. Is it really a hunger? Well, had you asked me in the moment, I'd probably have said, yes. Yet actually, looking back, it wasn't the need to satisfy a physical hunger that drove me to binge-eat. It was the need to devour, to consume, and to control some emotion or thought in that moment and the only way was to stuff something into my mouth. The more I ate, the less I felt the unsettling feeling and the more I felt in control. That was my reward for the insane act of overeating.

If you are feeling more in control and if the original thought or feeling that drove you into the kitchen is no longer significant, why then the purging? It is all about releasing, in a very volatile and final way, the thoughts and feelings you didn't want to think about in the first place. First you consume and devour the thoughts and feelings, via food, through your mouth. Then you have this extreme and intense need to rid yourself of the toxicity that you just consumed. It's not until all has been released from your system that you feel okay. By okay, I mean you feel calmer and no longer threatened by these thoughts and emotions and you can relax and get back to business.

If you have never experienced this or something similar, you must be thinking, Wow, that truly sounds crazy. And you would be correct in your assumption. For me, in the moment, it was the sanest thing I could do to survive the onslaught of thoughts and emotions that I was ill-equipped to handle.

This is just one example of what you can do to yourself and the choices that you can make while thinking you are doing so with total free will. In fact, some underlying force drives you to your choices and actions. You are SO not in free will or free choice when you have another force, other than you, driving you to a compulsive act. It's that force of those thoughts and feelings that drives you to live your life in a way that doesn't bring you joy and happiness.

What I'd like to do here is to help you understand, via self-evaluation, your actions that can either help or hinder your process in manifesting your heart's desires. First, ask yourself if your life is truly as you want it to be, with no exceptions and no doubts or regrets. If the answer is Yes, Yes, Yes, then you need not change anything. You have the understanding and the formula down pat. Congratulations! If, on the other hand, the answer is, I don't know or I'm not sure, or is an emphatic NO, then there is some deep soul-searching that needs to be done.

If you have a goal or desire in mind that you want to manifest AND if you feel you are doing everything correctly in trying to create it AND if it's not happening, then most probably you don't truly want to create it OR you are blocking or limiting yourself in some way. This could be due either to some unconscious thought or act or by some underlying emotion, such as fear or doubt.

My premise is this: If it's not broken, don't fix it, BUT if it's not working the way you want, something is wrong and needs attention. So, I say to you—no, better yet, I challenge you to look deeply into yourself and your life. Forget about anyone else's life. Look at YOUR life, and see what you are doing that may or may not be working for you. Where are you in need of changes and where are you completely satisfied?

Don't look outside yourself for the answers. You don't need to say, "If only he or she would..." or "If I only had more..." or "If I had been born into a different family..." or something similar.

You would be wasting your time and energy trying to figure out why someone else wouldn't or didn't do something or whether God had or hadn't given you better opportunities. In my world, these are called EXCUSES and excuses are like crutches. They don't let you walk tall and be strong and be the creator of your life, your dreams, or your world.

Following the self-evaluation, it is important to be honest with yourself and stop blaming other people or situations for you not fulfilling your dreams. The only person who is responsible for your life as you have it is you (excluding minor children or mentally or physically challenged individuals). When you realize and accept this, you can then be truly and totally in control of your life and what happens to you. This is the principle behind the eight steps of manifestation: Whether consciously or unconsciously, you create your reality, not someone else.

Let's say you consume more calories than you burn. The result would be that you gain weight. If you are a couch potato, you probably have flaccid muscles. You commit a crime, so you stand a good chance of being arrested. You are rude and insensitive to people, and you alienate yourself from them. The list can go on and on yet it always starts with you.

Even if you feel you have done nothing to warrant an attack, you can set yourself up to be attacked by doing, or not doing, specific things. For example: You marry a violent and abusive individual. You are then setting yourself up to live in a volatile environment where violence will prevail. No one forced you to marry or remain married. You did so for your personal reasons. If one of those reasons was that you loved that person and you felt he or she loved you, know that physical violence of any kind is not LOVE.

Or let's say you are going to a party but don't want to wait for a ride and decide to walk by yourself at night. You are afraid but go anyway because you are too impatient to wait. Do you think that you may be setting yourself up for a possible attack, especially if you have to walk through a rough neighborhood? I'm not implying that you may be responsible if there were an attack. What I'm saying is that you are not being sensible in your choices and are increasing the chances of violence being done to you.

If you are an alcoholic and want to quit drinking, don't go to a bar and, whatever you do, don't get a job working as a bartender or at a place where they serve alcoholic drinks. You would be making choices that would not assist you in staying out of danger and feeling safe or staying sober. You be the judge and be honest with yourself. Look at your life and see where you've made certain choices that have helped create your life as you now have it. When you can do this, then you are on your way to being a conscious creator of your life.

The word "conscious" is a big factor in your creation. Do you have to be conscious to create? No, but if you are, then you can have what it is you truly want. Be conscious, be responsible, be yourself. Make your choices with a free will and with the intent and the knowledge that you can create and are the creator of your life. Don't let someone else be the pilot of your plane.

Connect with the Divine Intelligence within you, God, or the Universe, and begin your co-creation. Don't live life as a victim. Live life as if you are your own creator, your own king or queen. You call all the shots. You are also responsible for all the shots being fired, both the ones hitting the bull's-eye and the ones that miss. You CAN have it your way.

Chapter Three

Conscious Manifestation

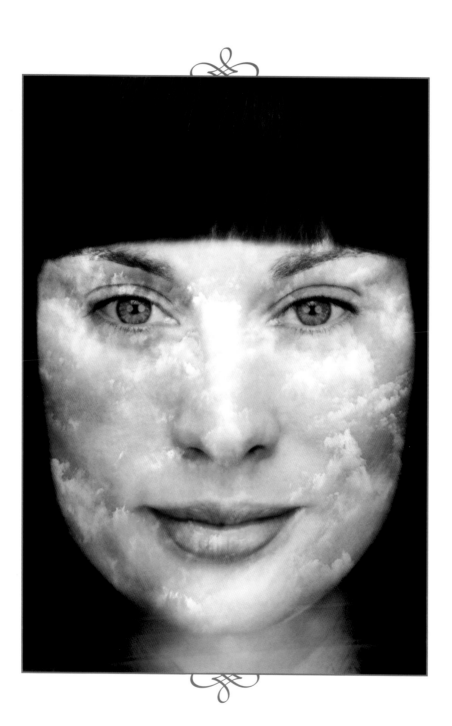

Focus on
Your Intent

– Three –

Conscious Manifestation

When you choose to live in your own world and to ignore the world around you, what happens? This is the part of manifestation—conscious manifestation—that I would like to focus on now.

If you were in a darkened room and couldn't see the sun rise or set because the blinds were drawn and because it also happened to be a gloomy day, do you think the sun would still rise and set? Do you feel that a baby misses his or her mother when the mother leaves the room and closes the door? Would your answer to these questions change the outcome? No, it would not. The earth still travels around the sun and there is a sunrise and sunset whether or not you can see or experience it. Your opinion of the baby's absence from his or her mother doesn't change what the baby is truly feeling.

Whether you choose to believe something is real, your belief doesn't change the results. The only thing that is affected by your beliefs is you. If you feel the sun has not risen, you may choose to stay in bed thinking it is still early and that you still need sleep. If you think the baby feels alone and abandoned, you would probably go pick up the child or go speak to the child's mother about her role as caregiver. All in all, the world is truly as you see it, at least to you. If you are asleep and dreaming of being chased by someone, the feeling of fear may enter your dream state, eliciting a dream image of you running. This may elevate your heart rate and you could possibly begin perspiring. Are you actually physically running? No! Are you actually perspiring and do you have an elevated heart rate? Yes! Does your body know the difference? No! The results are the same. The body responds to what you feel is real, whether it is real by other standards or not. Because the brain believed there was a real threat, the body responded by elevating the heart rate and increasing the body temperature.

Cellular biologist Bruce Lipton, Ph.D., discovered some phenomenal results during his research of causative factors of disease in the human body. His premise was that if you inherited a cancer gene, then you would be born with cancer. He found instead that while there is a genetic correlation to disease genetics don't determine whether you get the disease or not. He found, through cellular research, a stronger causative factor for disease—the environment. Even greater than environment, he discovered that your belief system is the strongest influence in determining disease. You, the person with the human body, decide whether you are going to switch on or off the disease mechanism within your body. It's that simple. I say, "If you are conscious and remain conscious, you can then determine the state of your health!"

I was not privy to Dr. Lipton or his work until approximately a year ago. I came to understand the relationship between health and disease during a healing crisis in my life, which I'll cover in detail in chapter nine. Suffice it to say here that what Dr. Lipton discovered years ago aligns with my inner beliefs and personal experiences on what causes disease.

YOU decide whether to turn on the switch for disease or to keep the switch turned off. I realize that this may be very diffi-cult to accept. I'm not here to preach or to convince you that you have to believe me to be healthy. I'm here to help you see life through my eyes and to see if maybe this might help you live a little more easily and joyfully.

This concept of being in control of your health can also be applied to other aspects of your life, relationships, career, or wealth. It applies to whatever you want to create within your life. I'm not trying to minimize or simplify your situation in life. I'd like to show you another way that may possibly help you make your life be a little more easy, more fluid and joyful. That's what I feel. You are here to help educate, inspire, guide, and assist others in this journey of life, to be the best that you can be with the least amount of struggle and greatest amount of joy and abundance.

If I don't have the answer, I love and appreciate the advice or guidance from someone who may have an "insight" into the answer. It's all about sharing what you know and working in tandem to create a unified group, a team.

You have something specific only to you that only you can share with others. So now I ask, what are you doing with your experiences, your knowledge, and your life that could possibly be shared with others? I'm not saying that you need to write a book or give a lecture. What I'm suggesting is that you speak your truth as much as you can and as often as possible. If someone is struggling and you see the problem, why don't you throw out the seed of knowledge that just may be the missing piece of his or her puzzle? It's like throwing out apple seeds and hoping that the seed will take root and grow an apple tree. The only thing to be careful about is not getting attached to the person getting the kernel of knowledge. Staying attached to the outcome borders on meddling.

Give from your heart and intellect to who you feel may benefit from your area of expertise and hope and pray that it makes their lives easier and freer of discomfort. No one likes to see people suffer. Do your part in your world of growth and evolution. Take time to heal you so you then can radiate this energy to the world to help heal others. Be the beacon of light for yourself. Shine your light over the paths of others so that they can find their own inner light.

Don't be afraid to stand out. Don't be afraid to make waves. Don't be afraid to make a statement. Don't be afraid to take a chance. Don't be afraid to make a mistake. Live in the light, in love, in the knowledge that you are on the right path, for you, and that no one but you truly knows what is right for you.

Often, when you have too many choices or get too much advice, it's difficult to know what to do. It's like the little child in the candy store not knowing what candy to pick with all the hundreds of choices being presented. Your options are many. Take the time to prioritize in your life and begin with one or two very important factors that you'd like to see change in your life.

I strongly feel there is no one RIGHT choice, but multiple possibilities. I believe that each choice or possibility takes you down a different path to the same goal. Sometimes you get there faster, with less effort and fewer detours. Sometimes you'll encounter more of a struggle. There is no one path that is right or wrong. There are different lessons to be learned on the way. If you've chosen a slower path, one with difficulty, perhaps with more experience and wisdom, you'll choose differently next time around. Again, there is no right or wrong, only different paths.

What can you do to prevent yourself from choosing the same path, only disguised, over and over? That is harder to answer than you'd think. Of course, you say to yourself, I'll never do THAT again, whatever that is, and then you find yourself right back in the same scenario doing the same thing and you've done it before you see the similarities. Why, you ask? The answer has much to do with your awareness of why you've chosen that path in the first place. That underlying factor I've spoken about, the unconscious energy or force that compels you to choose things not of free will, such as fear, doubt, guilt, is at work. Until you understand the why or learn the lesson or transform the dynamics, you will continue to have difficulties in this area of your life.

Each time you get the chance to choose and you choose the same scenario, the lessons become harder and generally more life threatening, especially if you are on a spiritual path. The reason I say this is because your soul, your spirit, has committed to growth and will not let you down or let you give up. The continuous knocking at the door of your consciousness gets stronger and more intense until, hopefully, you'll get it and CHANGE! Your life often needs to become so intolerable that you have no choice but to change.

As in Newton's law of motion, the force to move an object needs to be unbalanced to or different from the object to elicit a change and create movement. If you look at your life in this way, you'll see just how difficult it is to change. To learn a lesson or to become motivated to change, especially when the resistance to change is extreme, usually means that the benefits you will receive following the change will be great. If the change is truly what you want, then it is relatively guaranteed that the change will have phenomenally positive results in your life.

It's helpful to look at resistance to change in your life as an opportunity to create something wonderful. Don't look at it as a burden or as something that needs to be overcome. See it as a gift to change things in the way you truly want. Look at all things as gifts and blessings in your life and opportunities to improve your life.

I once had a male patient who had a disease called Guillain-Barre. It's a neuromuscular disease of unknown origin that can, and often does, attack every nerve and muscle in the body, rendering the person totally paralyzed and unable even to breathe on his or her own. This man arrived at the hospital very weak and soon required a respirator to assist with his breathing. He was married, the father of two preschool-age children, and he was paralyzed. He was the sole financial support for his family. He was dealing not only with a potentially life-threatening disease, but also with the inability to feed and clothe his family. His wife did not work and she didn't drive a car. This man, on so many levels, had been given so many obstacles in life and the mere automatic process of breathing, which you may take for granted, was also taken away from him.

This was a man I developed a close working relationship with as I treated him daily over a period of several months. He advanced to the place where he could move his muscles, sit and stand with assistance, and breathe on his own. His rehabilitation was lengthy, intense, and difficult at times, yet he never once said, "No, I can't." He dedicated his life to living and to improving his physical condition. His wife taught herself to drive and came to the hospital daily with the children.

At some point, to meet his expenses, my patient began painting still-life pictures of fruit on small blocks of wood. He sold them to the hospital personnel, who happily purchased them. As time went on, he became extremely creative and very accomplished with his paintings. Along with the success of his paintings he regained all muscle strength and nerve function, which does not occur with all Guillain-Barre patients. He became quite strong and "buff." He discovered he loved exercising and loved the way it made him look and feel. Prior to his illness, he had an eight-to-five job in an office and rarely exercised. After a time he no longer required rehabilitation and continued to physically improve on his own.

He came in to see me a few years later to say that he had not gone back to his office job and had continued with his painting and art. He and his wife owned two art shops. He very proudly told me that he had bought his wife a Cadillac. Wow! What a success story, and it all originated from a potentially life-threatening and debilitating situation. He was a man who had such extreme obstacles to survival and family security yet, once these were surmounted, he had created a life far more successful than he might have ever thought of or planned.

This story reflects the laws of the Universe. It is all about your perception of what a situation is and the choices you make around that situation. Here was a man who chose life, flipped the switch for the disease, and was able to create a life so much like a fairy tale that he had to come back to tell me how happy and grateful he was. Can you imagine what I felt to see this man again and to hear his wonderful news? His success and joy touched me very deeply then and does to this day when I think about it.

Another great way a person can turn his or her entire life around is through miracles, if you want to call them that. I had another patient, this time a two-week-old infant who had been born normal, yet contracted viral meningitis. The infant had lost all neuromuscular function and was paralyzed, considered literally physically and mentally challenged in lay terms. I saw this infant on a daily basis to help maintain increased circulation and joint flexibility, even though I was told by the physicians not to expect much, if anything, of this poor baby.

The mother was told that her child was not expected to improve and not to have false hopes. She was also told to consider looking for an institution in which to place her baby. She was devastated, yet continued to bring the child in to see me daily. She refused to accept the negative scenario as a possibility.

As I worked with the child, I instructed the mother in specific exercises for strengthening, stretching, balance, and coordination and advised that she continue working with the child at home. At some point, I felt the need to relay to the mother that I strongly felt this child was going to recover and that she should continue working with her child as if all was or would be normal. I told her to have trust and faith that all would work out. The mother was relentless with her child's rehabilitation program.

She believed and knew, on a very deep level, that her child was going to be fine and normal. Well, wouldn't you know, her baby began showing signs of muscular strength, balance, and coordination? It got to the point that the child was developing so well that the mother no longer needed to bring her child in for therapy.

Many years passed and I had moved out of town. I returned home for a family gathering and happened to be coming out of church one Sunday morning and heard my name. It was the mother of this baby, whom I hadn't seen or heard from in many years. She came over to me, grinning from ear to ear, holding the arm of a teenager. She introduced me to the teenager, her grown child. She wanted her child to meet the woman who had told her, 18 years earlier, that her child would recover. She also wanted to thank me and to let me know that I had given her a glimmer of hope. It was the thread that she held on to while she chose a normal life for her child. Not only was her child not disabled, yet had graduated from high school and had been an honor student. Wow again! See what you can do when you make up your mind that you want to create something, especially something that all signs indicate is impossible? The greater the obstacle is, usually the result is an even greater reward. That's how I see it and I'd love you to see it that way too.

Chapter Four

Embodying Your Power and Making a Difference

Embrace Your Inner Power

– Four –

Embodying Your Power and Making a Difference

*U*nderstand and believe that you are powerful. If you are not feeling that way right now, know you can be powerful when you choose to be, when you are ready. Inner power isn't about how much weight you can lift or how fast you can run. It's about accessing the unlimited power and knowledge from the Universe. It's the limitless power that comes through love and tapping into your Divinity. You can equate it to having an army by your side, your own group of advisers, with all the information you need right at your fingertips. Knowledge truly is power. Your only limitation is not realizing that it's there to tap into anytime you need it.

Have you ever been so physically and emotionally exhausted that you felt you couldn't walk another step or do one more thing, for fear you'd collapse? Somewhere, somehow, you managed to draw on an inner strength or power and you got the job done. Well, this is partially what I'm talking about. That strength comes from somewhere other than your physical being. It can't be measured. It can only be demonstrated by results.

Here's another scenario: You've worked very hard, it's late, and your children need to be fed. Your spouse also needs some special attention. You have a report due the next day and you need a massage because your body has been taxed to its limit. You feel you just need a private space and alone time, as you are on the verge of cracking. Somehow, after you've spent a few moments alone and have calmed yourself (following prayer or meditation), you get it all together and all needs are met, including your own. That's what tapping into your power is all about.

Have you ever been in a situation where you felt a sense of helplessness and thought that you couldn't handle things alone? Then somewhere or somehow, a sense of peace and calm replaced the fear and anxiety and you felt strong and confident that all would be well. If this has ever happened to you, then you've tapped into your inner power and guidance. You knew what to do next and were given an assurance that all is well now and will be in the future. It is, on so many levels, so simple and yet SO strong in its ability to give you the power to set thoughts into motion. You go from fear to love with the peace, calm, and clarity that is so important for manifestation.

People have been known to perform superhuman tasks when someone they love, particularly their children, needed help. They can lift heavy objects like a car, run into a burning building to rescue a loved one and come out unscathed. These superhuman feats often take on a supernatural or otherworldly quality and are not easily explained.

What about the father who awakens from a deep sleep to check on his two young children and discovers that one of the children has just that moment set the mattress on fire? Somewhere from within that wellspring of knowledge and power came a resounding wake-up call. This actually happened to someone I know and he mentioned to me that never before or since had he felt compelled to check on his children in the middle of the night. His children are now all young adults. So you tell me, what is that inner voice, that inner power that is available and accessible to all of us?

Why is it that sometimes you feel that you do not have access to your inner power? Actually, you always have access. It's often not knowing how to tap into it that prevents you from accessing what you need. Or sometimes you can be in an emotional state that doesn't allow you to make the connection to your inner guidance.

Your inner power is like a muscle. The more you use it to its capacity, the stronger and more flexible it will become. The more you tap into it and see the results, the more you will begin to trust it. The more you trust it, the more you will tap into and use it. It's a cycle and you need to decide how to get the cycle in motion. Just jump in and let the cycle begin!

Please don't wait until you are at a point of crisis to see whether you have the power and the know-how to overcome a problem or obstacle. It most certainly will work during those situations, yet if you are in sync with your inner power and your inner guidance, chances are greatly reduced that there will even be a crisis. Isn't that the way you would like to live your life: conscious, alert, fully functional, and in control of your life with an unlimited reserve of power, strength, love, and knowledge? I choose to live life in love, free from fear, with the inner knowledge that I could utilize all the universal power to assist me in accomplishing my goals in this lifetime. What would you choose?

What if you feel that you don't have that choice to make? What if you feel that life has passed you by? What can you do? These are great questions and ones that most of us have asked ourselves at some point in time.

If you are feeling that life has passed you by, ask yourself this: is it because this is the actual truth or is it that you might feel depressed, sad, or angry? People often can't see the wonderful things they've accomplished and instead seem to dwell on the things they haven't accomplished. You can be your own worst critic and you can be your own best cheerleader, too. If given the choice, why set yourself up for disappointment? Who wants to put time, energy, and money toward something that doesn't feel fulfilling and satisfying? Not too many people, I would guess. With this attitude, how can you feel motivated to discover or clarify your purpose in life? How could you imagine that you could ever make a difference in this world?

Everyone is here on this planet for a reason and it's up to you to find that reason. You can spend a lifetime looking for THE reason, any reason, for being here and not come up with an answer that satisfies you. You are here for YOUR specific reason and not for someone else's, so it is you who need to understand the reason for your existence.

Let's see if there can be some light shone on this area of your life. Let's see if you can identify your purpose in life and under-stand how you can make a difference. Help me to help you see your inner light and all the magnificent things you've already done for yourself and those around you. Let me help you open your eyes and your heart to see and feel who you really are.

Imagine yourself moving through life with mirrors held up in front of your face. Those mirrors are reflecting all aspects of you. You are seeing, reflected in these mirrors, all your emotions, thoughts, and actions. You can see yourself from all angles, showing the good side and the bad side. It's all here, all of you in Technicolor, on the big screen and with five-to-one surround sound. You see it all, hear it all, and are creating the movie as you travel through your life.

Some days you feel and look magnificently beautiful and notice that everyone seems to be smiling at you, holding the doors open for you, asking if they can be of assistance and just wanting to be around you, almost as if you had some magic energy or charm that they hope will rub off on them. On these days, you feel magical and you see this magic reflected in the eyes of those around you. People hang on your every word. They want to mimic your actions and even want to dress like you.

So, what is it that's happening around you? You, your energy, and your essence are being reflected back from the mirrors being held up by those around you. You are being shown aspects of who you are through the actions and responses, the mirrored eyes of those around you. You are not seeing others, per se. You are seeing yourself through their eyes. That is called instantaneous feedback.

If you can visualize that other people are your weather vanes that reflect back to you what's going on with you, then you'll have a very good point of reference to correct your course or continue down your path.

Now, have I thrown out a bit of food too difficult to swallow? Let me explain a bit further with a very simple example of how others reflect aspects of you. Have you ever picked up an infant child felt a little scared or apprehensive as to whether the child would remain calm or begin to cry in your arms, particularly if the child wasn't yours? As you begin to pick up the child you can see some fear and apprehension in the child's eyes. The moment the transfer is complete and the baby is in your arms, the crying begins. Do you think this has anything to do with you and how you were feeling prior to picking up the baby? More than likely, it does.

Children, in particular, are excellent barometers and will tell you almost immediately how they are feeling in any particular situation. Do you think that if you were comfortable holding babies, ALL babies, and that you knew how to console and calm a baby, that the baby would have begun to cry? I would say probably not. The baby picked up on your feelings of fear and apprehension and mirrored back to you what you were feeling.

At the same time, a child will be one of the first to reflect back to you your love and heartfelt joy. That's why so many people love the beauty and presence of the innocent. It's just that—the innocent, pure, and undisturbed response of a child with no agenda, no judgments, only reflective emotions.

That is why I, so many times in my life, have depended on feedback from my two sons, particularly when they were younger. I could trust that whatever they were reflecting back to me via their actions and emotions was generally on the mark. It often was the sole external feedback I needed in order to correct my path or change my ways. Conversely, it was excellent feedback, telling me that I was a very good and loving mother. It goes both ways. It told me both when I was off-course and when I was on the right path.

Here is where I'm going to challenge you to look deep within yourself and to think back through your life, to remember how you affected others in your life. Use their reactions to you as your mirror of how you were perceived by them. Concentrate only on the positive for now. The reason I say this is because you, I'm pretty confident, may have already beaten yourself up for the pain or heartache you felt you have caused others. It's time to let it go and forgive yourself, with the understanding that you are not consciously going to continue doing it.

Make a list of the expressions of love, joy, peace, friendship, gratitude, and appreciation that you've experienced with others throughout your life. Take a moment to look at your list. What is this telling you? It's saying that you are indeed a good person who has affected many people's lives and who has most probably been instrumental in helping others change their lives for the better.

How many times do you remember someone smiling at you or laughing with you? How many times has someone thanked you just for listening? How many times do you remember someone hugging you with deep love?

Have you ever helped someone overcome an insecurity or fear and seen them reach out to the world with their newfound self-image? How you taught someone else a special talent that you possess—like how to play a musical instrument, sing, dance, cook, knit, run, ride a bicycle, play a sport, read a book, think out of the box, speak a word in another language, open his or her heart to love?

Are you getting the picture? You are an individual unlike any other and your mark in life can be quite profound and permanent, so look at yourself as a teacher, a role model. You are someone of importance who contributes much to humanity, consciously or not. If you can allow yourself to be more conscious, then you will be able to multiply and magnify your gifts and direct them more consciously to people and places in need of your assistance.

Let's say that you have a special gift with animals. You feel that you understand them and on some level can communicate with them. You have great empathy for their situation and they trust you. Don't you think or feel that possibly you could use this gift you have with animals to help them? You could teach the rest of us humans the special secrets you may possess that could help us communicate better and more lovingly with our animals. What about volunteering or working for organizations that deal specifically with animals? The zoo, the Humane Society, animal conservation groups are just a few examples.

Suppose that you don't have a college education, don't feel very intelligent, or don't feel that you have any special gifts to share with anyone? I say to you that if you look more closely within yourself, you will not only find something to share with others, you will probably uncover something very great and special. Maybe you are a kind and loving person who lives life with your heart open and is always the first one to extend a hand in greeting. Perhaps you are someone whom a crying child will come to for comfort or whom a neighbor can count on for commonsense advice. Let's say that one of these individuals was literally helpless, in that moment, and that without you, he or she might not have chosen to continue on with life. How many times do you think that your loving smile brightened someone's day and provided a reason to keep on living? What do you think this means? You are important, you do make a difference, and you exude the divine light inside you.

No one goes through this life without making some sort of impact on others, consciously or otherwise. So why don't you make more conscious choices with your life, evaluate your talents and gifts, and see how you can share them with others? Sharing helps you in opening yourself to receive blessings in your life, and allows you to help many others who wouldn't be blessed if not for your participation in their lives.

Be aware of what you want, what you want to create, and what you want to contribute in this life. Once you have all this in mind a little more clearly, then DO something about it. You may be sitting on a gold mine of information, gifts, and talents that others are longing to experience and understand.

P.S. Don't forget to smile and reach out to others. We all need a little more sunshine in our lives.

Chapter Five

Co-Creation Through Manifestation

Discover Your Gifts

– Five –

Co-Creation Through
Manifestation

*L*et's concentrate on your inner beauty and gifts. I want you to understand the true essence of your humanity. I want to make sure you realize that you are a spirit living in a human body, not a body that happens to have a spirit living within. There is a great difference between the two.

Picture yourself in a car, driving down the highway. Would you say you are the car that happens to be carrying your human body inside or would you say that you are a human being who happens to be driving the car? I would feel safe to say you'd say the latter statement is true. You are a human being who happens to be driving the car. It's the same dynamic relationship you have with your spirit. You might think that because you cannot see your spirit, your body is the prime reason for existence. If you truly believe that, then I suggest you expand your vision to a much higher level and see the real purpose of your existence. Is it not because you have come here as spirit born or incarnated into a human body (your vehicle), to learn and evolve through the five senses, your body and mind? What a concept!

By now I've either piqued your curiosity or trashed any cred-ibility I may have had and you may be thinking I'm some type of radical, spiritual, offbeat individual who lives in her head with fantasies and illusions! Offbeat? Yes, I may be. Spiritual? Yes, I am. Radical? It depends on who's evaluating. Do I live in my head? When I became a left-brained intellectual, yes. Do I live in a fantasy? A resounding no! I live in the real world and that world involves my connection with the Divine, with heartfelt emotions, intuitive insight, inner knowing, and miracles. This is not a fantasy. Fantasies are imaginary, and what I know and what I've experienced are real, concrete, and documented events. They are not fairy tales that only sound good and make you feel good. They are real, and real not just by my standards.

What type of life would you be living if you felt you had access to immeasurable and supernatural powers? Probably a little different from what you're living now, correct? I would love you to see this power and beauty that resides within you, that is innately yours, that is your birthright, and that remains yours eternally.

No one can take the light away from you. It will remain with you until death. Let me give you an example: You see a magnificent pine tree, an evergreen, growing in your community. You marvel at its beauty, strength, and power, and its ability to remain green even during the darkest, coldest winters. During the spring the acorns drop and connect with the ground. A gestation period begins and then gradually, in time, you notice young pine trees beginning to form around the parent tree. Each young tree develops its own root system. Each is independent yet interdependent with the parent tree and each other, via the root system and the soil. Don't you think that each tree carries the same genetic configuration of the parent and carries part of the parent tree within it? If it weren't for the parent tree, it would not exist, correct? This genetic transference from parent tree to offspring correlates to your connection with God, the Divine. It's in your being for life.

It is your innate right to have and develop this inner light, beauty, and power. It's your connection to the Divine, your God, or cosmic force. For those who don't believe in a Supreme Being, whatever name you'd like to call this power that is greater than you (your Higher Power, your Yahweh, your Great Spirit, the Buddha, Allah), it is such an integral part of you. Without it you wouldn't exist.

Whether you believe the earth is turning on its axis and the sun rises and sets, these events are still happening. Whether or not you believe there is a divine force that's operational in your life doesn't stop it from functioning. The drawback to your not believing, the way I see it, is that you're not recognizing and harmonizing with your divine inner beauty and power, so you are not fully able to utilize its force in your life. I consider this a great waste!

Let's say you are athletic, intelligent, and old enough to ride a bicycle, yet you don't know how. What do you think might be the problem? Well, it could be as simple as the fact that you've never seen how a bicycle works and no one has ever taught you the basic mechanics of its use. You could have all the marvelous light, beauty, and power within you, yet not be aware of it or know how to use it, simply because no one has explained to you or shown you how to access it.

This is part of my purpose in writing this book—to help you to see this inner beauty, light, and power that reside within you. My purpose is to help you understand it, tap into it, and utilize it in your life for yourself and others. It is to help build a community of divine beings linking you to others, as the root system does with the pine trees. You are created to live with others in communities, and to work and play together, loving and supporting each other. Like the famous John Donne poem says, "No man is an island." I feel this is so true.

I want you to know, in a deep place within you, that you are never alone in this world. Even when you are not connected to any other human being on a physical level, you are still not alone. You are connected to your Divine, THE DIVINE, and this connection is with you throughout your existence. The Divine provides the inner strength that allows you to keep moving forward when you feel you can't take another step. It is what provides the inner strength to get up in the morning and to go to work even though you are feeling sad, miserable, and emotionally tired. It is the inner strength to keep going even though you've just come out of a bad marriage, yet know you have to keep moving because you are the sole support for your children. Think about all the times you've prayed for help and received it in the form of healed relationships, renewed health, or lifted financial burdens. How many times have you received answers to difficult questions or seen new career opportunities and situations opening up for you? You have tapped into your inner Divinity.

Let me give you another example of my inner Divinity connecting with another person's inner Divinity to help manifest or facilitate a miracle. This occurred three and a half years ago within my immediate family. My mother's older brother, who was 85 at the time, had an abdominal aortic aneurism that had been diagnosed three years earlier. He was told that it could rupture at any point, and more than likely he would die instantly with no time to make it to the hospital for a successful surgery.

You may be asking yourself why he didn't have elective surgery and have it repaired before it ruptured. It wasn't that easy. My uncle had been told that due to his age, as well as the fact that he had had two heart attacks and an abnormality in one of his heart chambers, the chances of surviving an open-heart surgery were slim. He had been evaluated and treated by two teams of cardiologists who verified this.

So, my uncle lived his life for three years with an underlying fear that he could die at any moment, with no warning signs of a rupture that could prompt him to go to the hospital. Then one day my cousin, the son of my mother's oldest brother, arrived in town to visit our uncle. He was a young cardiologist, on staff at the

University of Texas Medical Branch (UTMB) in Galveston, Texas, a teaching hospital for medical students. He began a conversation with our uncle about a new technique and device used to repair this type of aneurism that could possibly save his life.

After a short time, my uncle decided he wanted to have the operation. Thus began communication between all the attending physicians and my cousin and the cardiology staff at UTMB Galveston. I was notified of my uncle's decision to have the surgery and was asked to come down (an approximately 300 mile drive) to help support my uncle's healing. Not only am I a licensed physical therapist, I am an ordained minister who specializes in hands-on prayer-healing. I incorporate meditation and spiritual prayers into healings. I opted to go see my uncle before his trip to the Galveston hospital.

When I arrived and spoke with my uncle, I asked him to express his feelings about the surgery and allowed him to ask for my help in his healing. He, along with his team of physicians, greatly feared that the aneurism might rupture prior to the scheduled surgery. The plane ride might elicit just such a rupture. He and the physicians were now fighting a battle against time, hoping against hope that everything would remain stable until he went under the knife.

Now I had my work cut out for me. First, I cleared my mind and began my connection with my inner Divinity and called upon God to help me help my uncle to heal himself and to keep him stable during his travels to the hospital. My uncle was receptive to the prayer-healing and opened himself up to his connection with his Divinity, the same Divinity as mine, and together our bonded Divinity began the process of healing. He became very calm and almost fell asleep during the prayer-healing.

Initially I had my hands over the area of his abdominal aneurism and began visualizing a golden mesh of light weaving itself around it. During this process, I saw, through "internal sight," a strengthening of the aortic wall with this mesh of light. All of a sudden I got a strong sense that I should put my hands over his heart. It was such a strong impulse that I could not pretend it wasn't there, so for 20 minutes, I prayed over his heart. When I felt the urgency leave, I went back to the abdominal aneurism. The entire process lasted about 90 minutes. I then left and went back home.

I saw my uncle again, this time in Galveston, Texas, one week later when he was being admitted for testing. At the end of the first day of testing, my cousin, the cardiologist, entered the room to give us the results of the tests to date. He told us that, despite the phone conversations with my uncle's attending physicians and having received and studied all of my uncle's previous medical records, there must have been some great error along the way. From his testing he said that there was no evidence of any heart chamber defect or ANY signs of the two heart attacks that my uncle had experienced. Other than a slight thickening of the pericardium, the tissue surrounding the outside of the heart, which was common in a man of 85 years, there was no evidence of heart disease. Thus there was no apparent risk from the area of his heart. He said that my uncle's attending physicians MUST have made a mistake with the diagnosis.

Mind you, it had been three years since the diagnosis of his aneurism and all the while he was under the care of cardiologists and internists who were monitoring the progress of the size of the aneurism as well as the condition of his heart. So, knowing that there had not been a three-year mistaken diagnosis of my uncle's condition, I just asked my cousin a simple question. I already knew the answer, yet needed him and my uncle to hear and understand the seriousness of what had just happened.

I asked, "Could the scarring from a heart attack reverse itself?" My cousin's answer was a resounding NO. Once you have a heart attack it leaves a lasting impression on your heart for life, he said. I then told him that it must have been a miracle that healed him. Well, you can imagine what he said to me. He said it was impossible.

Needless to say, my uncle believed his heart had been miraculously healed. So began the process of my uncle periodically throughout the day and night asking for me to do my prayer-healing on him. It spread through the hospital like wildfire, that the uncle of one of the staff cardiologists had his heart miraculously healed by prayer. The physicians and nurses were privy to our prayer-healing sessions and were respectful of the process.

Suffice it to say that the surgery went extremely well for my uncle, and his abdominal aortic aneurism was repaired in two locations. The surgical physician opted to repair a second, unplanned and unexpected, aneurism. My uncle's heart was SO strong that the physician felt he could withstand the added length of time under anesthesia and the stress to his heart. The total time of surgery was nine hours.

My uncle lived three years after the surgery and just recently died at 88, of old age, and not due to a ruptured aneurism or heart attack. This goes to show you that when you tap into your Divinity, your powerhouse, and especially when you do it in conjunction with someone else, miraculous things can occur. Believe in yourself and your power to create the supernatural. This is the co-creation with your divine supernatural self, the God within you, which allows this to occur. Recognize it, trust it, and utilize it to do wonderful and miraculous things in your life.

Chapter Six

Male vs. Female:
The Roles Assumed by Each and What They Contribute

Understand and Embrace
Your Feminine Role

– Six –

Male vs. Female:
The Roles Assumed by Each and What They Contribute

*T*here is a woman in all of us—that is the feminine principle. The feminine is your receptive, grounding, and nourishing quality. It is the earthy quality strongly connected to manifestation. To manifest—to create—you must give birth to it through your feminine aspect. Acknowledge your feminine, embrace it, and utilize it to create your heart's desires.

I am speaking to men and women both when I talk about the feminine. There is masculine and feminine in all of us. The roles of the male and female, though, are not quite as cut and dried, not quite as clear as they once were. Nowadays, men and women work side by side in offices and fight side by side on the battlefield. The distinctions between gender-related roles barely exist. It wasn't always like this. Until the '40s and World War II, generally the woman stayed home and raised her children. She cared for and fed her family, all the while managing the home and household affairs. The man went to work, earned the money, and assumed responsibility for the welfare of his family. He usually didn't lift a finger to help his wife at home and was waited on hand and foot by her.

In those days men were doctors, lawyers, businessmen, manual laborers, military recruits, sports jocks; women were wives and mothers, secretaries, teachers, or caregivers.

Then came the feminist movement of the '60s, and everything began to change. Women burned their bras (I threw mine away, temporarily, in the '70s) and began protesting for better jobs and equal pay. They put their children in day care and entered the workforce. They began assuming what were described as male characteristics: They were more assertive, dominant, and less emotional. Women felt they had a right to demand equal rights with equal pay, disembodying the feminine/receptive and incorporating more of the masculine, action-oriented roles. This created some upsetting and unsettling situations between men and women in the workforce, and many changes began to occur.

It was, and may still be, mainly men who experienced confusion when women entered the workforce. Perhaps they were totally unprepared for the number of women who were coming in and didn't know just how they were going to handle competition for jobs or how to work with them as equals. This confusion spawned a generation of men who began losing touch with the identity of their male roles and began questioning where they were going to fit in. It even generated confusion as to how to behave on a date. Who was supposed to ask whom and who was going to pick up the tab?

The weakening of the male role as provider began and roles began to reverse. It wasn't unusual for women to work outside the home, earning wages, while more and more men were staying at home and becoming Mr. Mom. Family size decreased and some couples decided not to have children at all. Now many young adults are opting not to marry and are either living together as a couple or living alone.

What actually happened first—females demanding equal rights and jumping out of the feminine persona or males becoming confused and allowing females to compete for their role? I'm not sure it really matters. Each affects the other and both are responsible for shifts in society, the weakening of the family unit, and for much of the problems faced within relationships today.

Does a person possess the skills and role of one's sex by virtue of birth or is the role learned? I feel that it is a little of both. By virtue of genetics, people have certain likes and dislikes, mainly affected by hormones. Yet, I feel, much is acquired through one's environment, by example. One assumes and is conditioned to a mindset.

I was raised in a very conservative Catholic family, the youngest of five—three boys and two girls. In my family, the roles were very clear and there was no crossing the line. The girls were not allowed to go hunting with the older boys and our father. This was a MALE activity. Girls were not allowed to touch guns.

The boys were shown how to cut the grass when our gardener was off and my sister and I were taught to dust, vacuum, and do the dishes when our maid was off. I remember once, when I was around seven or eight years old, I wanted to go outside with my older brothers and help them cut the grass and was told that little girls didn't work outside and that only the boys could. What a shock this was! I couldn't understand the logic behind this, yet I accepted it as truth when stated by my parents.

Even though there were strict lines drawn between male and female roles, my mother, in many respects, was an early feminist and taught my sister and me never to depend on a man to take care of us. She would always say that we needed to be educated and independent and capable of supporting ourselves. She said that anything could happen within a marriage and, God forbid, that our husbands could die or worse yet, we would end up divorcing, and we would have to raise our children without the help of a man.

My mother was a very beautiful and feminine-looking woman, yet she had strong male qualities—she was dominant, insensitive, and non-demonstrative. She gave my sister and me mixed messages regarding what the female role was all about. On the one hand, she did wait on my father. On the other hand she would say and do things that would emasculate him. We heard one thing and saw much more of the other, all the while being told that females had a distinctive role to play in a relationship.

In Kabbalistic teachings (Jewish mysticism), as taught to me by the homeopath, Vega Rozenberg, the role of the male versus the female is quite distinctly delineated. The female role is described as the spiritual guide for her male counterpart, the one who brings them both back to God, the Divine. The male, on the other hand, although not as open and receptive to the Divinity, carries the highest light-frequency vibration (Divinity) within his body, his sperm. The female and her anatomy are revered and deferred to as the one more spiritually knowledge-able. It's her feminine/receptive quality that gives birth, and brings forth life.

According to the Kabbalah, the woman's role is to be the chalice, strong and firmly rooted in the earth, to receive the wine (light) from the man, who feeds her until her cup is overflowing. She then nurtures him back with her surplus. She grounds the light, creating the roots to his tree, allowing him to grow taller and closer to the Divine, all the while continuing to nurture her with his divine light.

Accumulation of wealth and abundance is considered the female role, not achieved by going out to work and procuring it, but by receiving it from her man and then grounding it into the physical earth. This in turn will perpetuate wealth (flowers and crops growing).

The male role is to be the protector, the provider, and keeper of the well-being of his woman and family. He also protects them from the ultimate enemy—disease—and it is his role to make sure that all is well within his family home.

Let me give you a couple of examples of how this universal principle works.

My father was born into a wealthy land/ranch family and when he married my mother he had much to offer her in the way of meeting her physical needs. My mother moved about 80 miles away from her family to marry my father and to be close to his ranch. After they had their first two children, both boys, my mother told my father that she wanted to move the family back to her original home and suggested that my father commute to the ranch. He conceded and so began the separation of the family. My father began to stay at the ranch during the week and came home on the weekends. My mother chose to be near her parents and sister instead of being with and supporting her husband, my father. She was no longer the female recipient of his energy and light (wine), no longer by his side to guide, advise, and support him. All his efforts fell on empty ground; her chalice was not available. The ranch began having multiple problems (theft, weather-related problems, mismanagement). Livestock was sold to meet the expenses. Eventually the land, excluding some of the mineral rights, was sold and the family was literally broke.

What had happened? My mother, the feminine within this relationship, didn't fulfill her role, and physical and monetary devastation occurred. Years later when my mother assumed the role of the breadwinner, as a science and math teacher, she became ill and required open-heart surgery (mitral valve prolapse). This time my father hadn't fulfilled his role as protector from enemies, in this case illness and disease. He had no more wine to pour into her chalice. The fountain was dry, and the result was illness of the feminine, my mother.

Following the surgery and during the recuperation, my father went into a state of emergency. He pulled out all his reserves and began overindulging my mother with everything he had—

love, prayers, care, and attention. He doted on her while she was in the hospital and slept in a chair by her bed. He didn't leave any stone unturned in nurturing her back to health. My mother recovered rather quickly and became a warm, loving woman, full of life and health. Thus began her receiving of my father's energy, love, and care. She took it all into her chalice (initially to help heal herself), and then began nurturing my father in return with the overabundance of love she received from him. What do you think happened next? Yes, the wealth began returning back to the family via land royalties. Was this a coincidence or a universal principle? You be the judge.

The flow of the Universe happens in its own sequence whether you believe it or not, so why not begin trusting it and learn to flow with it to create your life the way you would like? I'm not implying that you need to follow the paths of my parents. Just be aware of the principles of the male and female roles and make your choices accordingly.

If your life is working the way you'd like, then don't change a thing. If you're not happy with what's happening within your life, do something to change it. I've just revealed to you some universal secrets of how you can help yourself be and do what you've always wanted. You hold both male and female energies within you and it's the balancing of these energies that will determine how successful you are at creating your reality. Be your male protector and learn to take care of yourself. Be the female receiver and create what you want from life. It's all in your heart, mind, and soul.

Chapter Seven

Doing vs. Receiving

Become the
Feminine Receptive

– Seven –

Doing vs. Receiving

*I*ncorporating the feminine principle of being open and receptive while being in a passive role is what the universal feminine is all about. It is the state you want to assume in order to solidify your manifestation. So why is it that you often end up doing so much for so many? Women especially do a lot for their families, mostly their spouses.

In doing, you become the active, masculine force in a relationship. Therefore on some level, you are not allowing your partner or spouse to be the man. Isn't it supposed to be just the opposite? The male energy protects and provides for the family. He is to bring to you the wine for your chalice. He is to fill your cup to overflowing so that you can then nurture him back.

I was once told by a very wise woman, Kathleen Bittner-Roth, that men fall in lust with the different female archetypes, such as the mother and the playgirl, yet only fall in love with your feminine goddess. She went on to say that once a man falls in love with the goddess within you, that love is solid, concrete, and forever. She said that a man falls in and out of lust with the other female archetypes yet never falls out of love with your goddess. She told me that I personally needed to let the man be the man and let him do for me, particularly at the beginning of a relationship. Let him open doors, pay for my meals, pick me up, and take me out. I was not to lift a finger to do anything for him, not even offer to cook for him, at least initially.

Kathleen implied that this was the way I was going to understand the feminine principle and learn to better incorporate it into my life. She said that she felt it would be difficult for me to sit and do nothing, just to receive, since I am a very giving person and have a need to give. She said I was to sit on my hands before I attempted to do anything for a man and that I needed to do less talking and much more listening. Responses to his questions and statements were acceptable, yet overall I needed to remain quiet and listen. This is the feminine/receptive principle.

In time, once I decided that I liked the man and wanted to develop the relationship, I could begin doing small things for him, yet I would still need to allow him to be the predominant giver. Kathleen said that a man's reward for "doing" something for me was being in my presence, receiving my smile, my energy, and my light. She said that this was my gift to him and that I need not do more. Just as someone enjoys seeing and smelling a rose in bloom, so too should the man get enjoyment from experiencing a woman's essence. This was what I concluded from her conversation.

Well, you can imagine what I thought and felt listening to those words. How was I going to be in a relationship with a man, with anyone, and not be the giver? That seemed almost impossible to me, yet I did try it, on occasion, and noticed that when I was truly in the feminine/receptive role, things came to me effortlessly. People wanted to do things for me and give me things. People took the time to give me directions or give me their place in line when they saw that I was carrying something heavy. Also, what I did notice was that I seemed much more approachable and people smiled at me more, with more eye contact. Somehow I felt prettier and definitely more lovable and loving.

Kathleen was saying that I, as a woman, needed to understand and incorporate my feminine goddess energy. This in turn would help me attract a man who would be loving, attentive, and faithful and who would fall in love, not in lust, with me.

So why was it so difficult for me to embrace this concept and stop doing so much for those I loved? Why was I having problems allowing them to do things for me? Was it because I felt that on some level allowing others to do for me was being needy and weak? Or was it because I would then feel indebted or, worse yet, inferior? These are not uncommon thoughts.

We are taught at an early age that the female is the "weaker" sex and that females cannot do certain physical tasks as well as men. This is correct physiologically in most male/female relationships, yet the feminine energy is NOT weak. The sooner you truly understand this, the sooner you will be able to embrace the feminine within you and begin the process of creating and manifesting.

Crying is another external symptom labeled as feminine or childlike. Many call crying weak, and it's often thought of as a negative trait. Not so! Crying indicates the ability to release pent-up emotion. You can cry with compassion when you see a young child injured or when a loved one dies. This is not being weak. You are using your ability to flow the energy of sorrow and pain through you and out. It frees you to utilize your inner energy to focus in a direction you want to go. You won't be blocked. Blocked energy within the body not only decreases the ability to manifest or create what you want, it is also a precursor to disease. The more you flow your energy, your feelings, and your thoughts, the more flexible, strong, and healthy you can become. These are the rewards of being in your feminine flow.

Both male and female energies reside in you and the goal is to be able to balance these two polarities, allowing you to be everything that you need for yourself. There is a distinct function the feminine principle has within a relationship and that is to receive, ground, and nurture the energy given to her by her male counterpart. Don't be afraid or ashamed to open yourself to receive. You are not only in a vulnerable state by staying open; you are also in a position of strength and power. I say strength because you are able to receive the abundance from the Universe that allows you to co-create with the Divine.

Love and honor your feminine. Don't dishonor it by neglecting or ridiculing it. Somehow, this is a big issue for me. I seem to find myself in the position of over-giving, mainly to my children and my mate. There is a point at which I notice that the giving is very lopsided, and that is when I also notice a lack of attention or concern for me. The more I give, the more I feel is expected of me to give, and the less appreciated I feel. It's as if they aren't honoring me as a female. Actually, it's because I've not honored the feminine within myself. They are only responding to what I'm conveying.

So, why do I do this? Where and why do I get off-balance? Is it because loving and wanting others to be happy elicits this need in me to do for them and give to them? This, in and of itself, is not the issue. The issue for me is the imbalance over-giving creates within the relationship and the unhappiness and unfulfilled feelings that arise from it. So how can I stop and what can I replace it with?

Often if you can't find a solution to a problem, you need to disassociate yourself from the problem, at least for a short period, and for me that means to do nothing! In doing nothing, I am allowing myself to receive input from my inner guidance. This is another feminine principle that comes into play, listening to your inner guidance. Try it! Replace continual giving with an openness to receive and see if this helps balance out the energies of giving and receiving.

As you can see, whether you are a male or female, you use the feminine principle to operate within this world. Don't be afraid of it. Don't neglect it. Embrace it and be proud of it while allowing the feminine within you to flourish and grow.

Chapter Eight

Open Yourself
to Receive

Be Open to Receive

– Eight –

Open Yourself to Receive

When you choose to open yourself up to receive, following the feminine principle, you are also opening yourself up to feel. This is also feminine in nature. This is one of the requirements needed to manifest in the physical plane. When you are open to receive and feel, this also means that you can receive and feel pain as well as joy. Pain is something that you don't consciously choose to experience, yet it is often the necessary force needed to change your life to fulfill your heart's desires. I will explain this in a little more depth.

Initially, pain or the possibility of unpleasant experiences may cause you to shut yourself down to the point where you may become numb or block the pain or unpleasant feeling. This is a common survival technique, one I used as a self-protective measure when my second husband was beating me. In shutting myself down, I survived the situation at hand, yet limited my ability to manifest. Why? When the door is closed or partially closed, the energy is prevented from moving in or out.

In actuality, when you do feel pain or sorrow, even temporarily, it is often a good sign. It demonstrates that you are open, receptive, in tune with the appropriate emotion, in the moment. It means the energy is flowing. As long as you allow the pain or sorrow to flow through you and not get stuck, it will not limit your ability to manifest. You, in turn, are not being influenced, consciously or unconsciously, by something that you choose not to acknowledge. You can live life fully.

Pain, like unpleasant-tasting medicine, is a necessary evil, so to speak, to facilitate a cleansing or healing. It warns you that something is out of alignment. You have to go through the unpleasant experience, or at least acknowledge it, to be well. I'm not saying that experiencing your pain is the cure-all. What I'm saying is that by allowing yourself to acknowledge the unpleasantness of the pain, and then dealing with it and letting it go, you are truly learning to be in the flow. You are the captain of your ship. The moment your ship starts to take on water, you acknowledge that there is a problem and deal with what is creating this problem by bailing out the water. Then you remain aware and vigilant so it doesn't happen again. You are living consciously and responsibly.

If you can see and feel what's out there, then you are in control of the situation. Don't allow yourself to be only half-aware or half-awake. This is partial living. To be fully alive means that you are taking the chance that you will be able to deal with whatever comes into your life, the good and the bad. This is all about being in control of your life.

Conscious awareness is where you need to live to be able to utilize the tools of manifestation. If you are blind, then how can you read an instruction booklet? If you have no one around to read it for you, how are you going to be able to set up your computer, for example? The instruction booklet in this case would be the eight principles, or steps, of manifestation. These principles are a step-by-step guide that tells you how it all works. If you are not conscious enough to read and understand the instruction booklet, how can you then implement its principles? It all starts with being aware of and in touch with what's there in and around your life. Know what you want to keep the same and what you'd like to change.

Be open and honest with yourself about your life. Look inside yourself for the answers. You have a fountain of information just waiting to be accessed. Tap into your feminine intuitive side and see how easy it is to know the next step to take in your life.

Know that the deeper the connection you make with your inner guide, the more accurate your answers are going to be. You can go to a place within yourself where you feel total peace and calm and where you can experience the sensation of pure love and Divinity. This is where you will access the next steps. It is also where you will access the wisdom, power, and love that are innately yours from birth.

Do you think you were born here on earth without any map or guide to assist you with your life's journey? You are actually given a custom-made map, divinely placed in your DNA, your genetics, and in your heart and soul so that you can navigate your life. Listen to yourself. Pay attention to your intuition and to the signs your body, your heart, your intellect, and your soul send you. All you have to do is learn how to listen (a feminine principle), interpret the information, and then implement it. If you are out of balance and are more emotional than intellectual, spiritual, or physical, then your interpretation will be colored by emotion. This applies to all facets of your life.

Achieving and maintaining the balance within yourself is not always easy and yet it is an important factor in the way you manifest. Let's say you are an intellectual individual and you take pride in staying in control of stressful and potentially emotional situations. You consider yourself levelheaded and rational. Now you've decided that you want to share your life with a partner. You think that it would be nice to have a companion to grow old with. This is a very reasonable thought and desire and something you could definitely consider manifesting for yourself. There's just one factor that you've left out. Everything you've just conveyed is from the mind/intellect and didn't incorporate any emotionality (love), or spirituality (God), or physicality (gender, age, or sexuality). If all factors are not considered, you may end up manifesting someone who will fit the bill intellectually, yet lack the substance that is essential for a successful long-term union. That's why I say it's vital to be conscious of what you want. Self-evaluation may be necessary for a check-in on where you stand within the framework of your manifestation. If you manifest from an imbalanced foundation, the outcome of your desires, most probably, won't be exactly what you wanted.

The reason I'm putting so much emphasis on your consciousness is that being asleep or partially asleep limits your ability to manifest what you truly want from life.

No one wants to admit that he or she may be responsible for manifesting ill health, yet all signs point to the fact that you, the body, are just following the directives from the central command station, the brain. If you tell yourself to do something or to feel a certain way, your body simply responds to the command. It's as if your body is your computer and your mind/brain is the computer chip programmed to work in a certain manner. If your mind controls your body and your life, why not program your mind chip to elicit the exact response you'd like to create from your body?

You already know that on some level what you think will happen usually does happens. If you think you're pretty and act pretty, people will respond in kind. Have you ever asked yourself why people think a certain person is SO beautiful? When you analyze the facial features and body parts separately, there is no distinguishing feature that you can see, yet when you put them all together into one package they translate into beauty. Have you considered that possibly it's an energy or attitude that elicits a response in others? This person most probably radiates beauty from within and so you feel and see it.

Why not use this same principle to manifest what it is you TRULY want from life? Reprogram your mind, your internal computer chip, to the program you want to see or create in your life. It can be that simple. Try it. Turn what you don't want into what you do want. Turn no into yes. You have nothing to lose but the outdated programs that no longer suit your life, and you have everything to gain.

As the youngest of five children, I was told "no" quite a bit. In some odd, offbeat way, I can say that this was a blessing in disguise for me. The word "no" to me wasn't one of rejection or finality. It was a way for me to think of a better and more creative approach to present my request. I didn't take the answer "no" personally at all. I took it as meaning that for the time being I couldn't have it my way, but if I were to change what I wanted or waited a little longer, then maybe I could get it. If I were to broach the subject later, with a different approach, under different conditions, and with heightened sensitivity, maybe I would succeed and get what I wanted.

All in all, the "no" gave me more time and space to think out of the box, to be more industrious and more creative and to elicit help from others who could possibly assist me in the manifestation of my desire. This is another way of saying, "If at first you don't succeed, try, try again," but don't keep bumping into the same wall over and over again. Try something different. Think positively and you will create positive things for yourself.

Take the time to look at yourself and your life and try to enumerate all the times you've created EXACTLY what you wanted or were thinking about, good or bad. Go back to that time to look at what else was happening in you and around you to help facilitate that exact response. You will begin to see a pattern of how you, personally, manifest. When you become more conscious of your thoughts and actions, then you can be more in control of the path your life takes.

When you are in control of your life and the direction it takes, you will receive all the wonderful blessings that are yours for the receiving, not taking. This is a totally different energy and you need to know the distinction. "Yours for the receiving" means being in your open, feminine/receptive self, while "yours for the taking" incorporates the active, action-oriented masculine energy and denotes lack, not abundance. This is a very big difference! When you receive you add to your abundance and when you take, it usually is due to the absence of abundance. You make the distinction between what it is you want to create and how you choose to create it.

Open yourself to receive the wonderful blessings that are there for you to experience and embody. Be the feminine/receptive in strength, grace, and love. Follow your heart and divine inner guidance and allow yourself the gift of receiving. It is for you to embrace and to relish. Like the flower that opens to receive the sunlight, so too should you open and trust your feminine/receptive side.

Chapter Nine

Relationships

Nurture Your Relationships

– Nine –

Relationships

How many types of relationships are you in? There are many possibilities: personal, business, parent-child, spouse or lover, friend, self, to name just some of the primary ones. You are in a relationship with just about everything and everyone you come into contact with, whether human, animal, vegetable, or mineral. For example, not only do you interact with other human beings, you interact with your pets, birds in the sky, wildlife on the ground, insects all around you, and the minerals that you consume and absorb within your body, if only to form an opinion of them.

You relate to all things, animal, vegetable and mineral, in just about the same way. You relate with love, joy, and acceptance; with fear, animosity, and intolerance; or with neutrality. This may seem a little hard to believe. Take for instance the relationship humans have, especially females, with chocolate. Have you ever seen someone take a bite of chocolate, then melt into a gooey state of blissful calm and peace? Well let me tell you that it has happened to me more than once, too many times to count! I was actually approached by a woman in the cafeteria of a hospital where I happened to be working at the time, and was told that I was the focal point of her lunch as she watched me eat my piece of chocolate cake. She said that she had never witnessed ANYONE consume a piece of chocolate cake with such relish and enjoyment. She said that it was so moving that she had to come over and tell me. Well, you can imagine what was going through my head! What was I doing? What was I saying? Was I moaning or moving my body? What had I unconsciously revealed to this woman who seemed to enjoy the show totally? Most probably I showed signs of someone being totally satisfied on ALL levels, just from a piece of chocolate cake.

If your relationships apply in so many contexts, if they are so "generic," why do you think you'd have problems relating? Why is it so difficult to relate to and live in harmony with others who are like and unlike yourself? Why, if you relate generically to all things, influenced by preferences, do you have the most problems with those closest to you? This is the dilemma.

You may be asking yourself, what does this woman know about relationships? Who is she to tell me what relationships are all about? Well, let me say that I do know plenty about intimate, marital relationships. I've been there and done that, three times to be exact. I'm a woman who has taken many missteps, made some unhealthy choices, yet I am a woman who is more aware, informed, and educated about the world and relationships because of the wrong turns I've taken. Not only have I learned about the dos and don'ts of marriage, I've learned about the dos and don'ts of relating to myself. This is what it's all about. If you cannot truly accept, love, and cherish yourself, then it will be difficult to convey those qualities to others. This includes your spouse, children, family, friends, coworkers, and the general population as well as others of the animal, vegetable, and mineral kingdoms.

How do you account for the disharmony people have with themselves and food in general, for example? Why are there so many instances of eating disorders, from anorexia and bulimia to gluttony and obesity? I've been there and done all that in one form or another, including what some people call exercise anorexia: exercising to the point of exhaustion and excessive caloric burning where the body cannot maintain any added weight. I'd eat that piece of chocolate cake and begin obsessing about the caloric intake and then instantly begin planning to burn off those calories so I wouldn't put on any weight. This is as abnormal and harmful to you as someone who won't eat or someone who eats and then throws it all up or someone who overeats. They are just different sides of the same coin that you choose to manifest.

It's true: even an eating disorder is something you manifest, though often unconsciously. So if you are to be truly in control of your life and begin to create your reality the way you want, it is important to be aware of all aspects of your behavior in order to change it.

Have you ever arrived home from a party to find a piece of spinach or grains of cracked pepper between your teeth, or worse yet, the zipper to your pants partially open and no one has told you? This generally is very upsetting and humiliating! You might immediately begin to think about all the people you inter-acted with who could have seen it and your horror intensifies! You could also get home, notice the food between your teeth, take it out, and go on with your life. Or perhaps you don't care about having food stuck between your teeth or you really don't care about the condition of your teeth and you choose to leave everything as is. That's also a choice, but know that not too many people will warm to the idea of kissing you, especially not French-kissing you. If you are wondering why you are not being nurtured in this manner, then you may want to look at the food stuck in your teeth, not to mention the bad breath the decaying food can create. Yuck!!!

Relationships. So what happened in my relationships with my former husbands? You may be thinking that I don't believe in marriage or a committed relationship and I would have to say that is not the case—quite the contrary. I totally believe in the institution of marriage. I tried it three times because I truly wanted a loving, healthy, and intimate relationship with a man. Know that I was financially independent before, during, and after my marriages and that financial security was not the reason for any of my unions.

You may ask, why didn't the marriages work? Isn't the third time supposed to be the charm? Obviously, it was not for me. If I had to evaluate the three marriages, I'd have to say that the third and shortest of the marriages was the most devastating and potentially life-threatening for me. If I learned anything during my marriages and relationships, it is that if you don't learn the lessons the first time around, the second and third times get more intense and severe. It's as if the Universe isn't allowing you to stay asleep. It's God's way, your soul's way, of saying you're not going to be left alone or allowed to give up until you see the whole truth, which hopefully will help you make any needed changes. When this happens, then you can truly make your choices with a free will. I say this because oftentimes you make choices that you think are of your own free will, yet are choices that are really being controlled by some underlying emotional factor (fear, anger, hate, trauma, doubt). You do know by now that often those choices you make out of intense emotion come back to haunt you later, often bringing great regret because you realize it wasn't what you wanted to create in the first place.

With my three marriages, I was the one who attracted these men into my life and married them. No one forced me into these relationships, so I am the only one whom I can hold responsible for these marriages. Granted, I'm not condoning some of the actions of my husbands. For all intents and purposes some of their behavior would be considered unhealthy and not conducive to a working, committed relationship. On some level, I allowed this inappropriate behavior to occur in my marriages

and, whether I liked it or not, I admit responsibility for everything that happened to me, including the physical beatings I
received from my second husband. This was a very difficult fact
for me to understand and accept. I was responsible, in some
way, for the beatings. What I realized was that his behavior was
abnormal, unacceptable, and unlawful and I will never accept
his behavior as okay. I also realized that I didn't have to receive
those beatings. On some level, by not doing anything, I was
allowing them to keep happening. I was responsible for my
behavior, not his. By not responding or defending myself, I
assumed the victim role and became emotionally paralyzed. I
"zoned out" and froze my emotions so I wouldn't feel.

Where was this coming from? Why did I, Ms. Independent,
Ms. Intelligent, and Ms. Adventurous, allow this to happen?
There were many questions left unanswered as husband
number three came along.

This is the one relationship that I have a difficult time
recounting. The first two husbands are still in periodic contact
with me and we have amicable relationships. All is resolved and
forgiven. Husband number three is the one I try not to think of,
yet the journey that I traveled with him was probably the most
profound and transforming of my life. This is where I created for
myself a life that resulted in two potentially life-threatening
illnesses. It is the relationship in which I discovered my inner-
most strength and the power of self-healing. It was through this
relationship that I discovered that when I was out of alignment
with my life, my body began to break down and disease set in.
Prior to this, even through the physical beatings, my body
remained healthy and resilient. My ability to freeze and not feel
the pain would be considered remarkable by most standards. I
could block out physical pain as if it didn't exist.

Two weeks prior to the breakdown of my physical body,
during my third marriage, I had called a friend from out of town

and mentioned to him that I felt my soul was dying. I couldn't describe it any other way. It was a feeling that I had never remembered experiencing before. It felt as if something very deep inside me was losing strength and as a result, I felt lifeless. There were no physical symptoms that I could describe to anyone, just this inner feeling of dying. Consciously I didn't want to die. I didn't want to kill myself, yet this feeling of dying was SO present that I couldn't shake it.

Besides mentioning it to my friend, I didn't know what to do with this feeling. I was, in spite of my experiences in life, a very optimistic person, so for me this feeling was foreign. Did it bring up any fear? No, not really. I guess I was past the emotional state and had gone to some uncharted territory. Not knowing what this feeling was all about, I just sat with it until the day came two weeks later when I discovered that I had developed a serious illness. Forty-eight hours after that, I discovered that I had developed a second potentially life-threatening illness.

At this point I realized, in a state of complete calm, that I had a death wish and that on an unconscious level I no longer wanted to live my old life. Did I really want to die? This is exactly what I asked myself and the answer I received was a big, fat NO!!! I did not want to die then or anytime soon. Thus began the process of understanding the power I had within myself to change my reality, which at the time was a state of illness, to a state of health.

I invoked all the strength from within myself and made a conscious choice to live. I heard myself cry out loud, "God, I don't want to die, please let me live!" So, for 18 consecutive hours, I prayed, pleaded and cried, all the while choosing life. I then drifted off to sleep. When I later awoke, I knew, on a VERY deep level, that I was fine and that I no longer was sick. How did I know? It was a strong, intense inner knowing that all was well with me and in my world. The peace and calm that I experienced only confirmed that all was fine. Let me just say that I do believe in miracles, so for me to go from a state of illness to a state of health in just 18 hours was perfectly normal for me in my world of miracles.

You may be wondering what these two potentially life-threatening illnesses were that I keep referring to. The first one was hepatitis. I was diagnosed the week before Christmas. I awoke one morning feeling extremely drained, tired, running a high temperature. I noticed, when I went to the bathroom to wash my face and brush my teeth, that I was completely yellow. Being olive-complexioned, I looked very closely at my face and eyes to make sure and there was no doubt in my mind that I had hepatitis. My face and corneas were completely yellow.

I immediately went to the hospital. I was examined and was told that it looked like I had hepatitis and that I needed to see a specialist the following day. I went to an internist the following day that drew blood and ran multiple tests for hepatitis A, B, and C. He suggested that I advise everyone that I had been in contact with during the previous week to get a gamma globulin shot that would help protect him or her from contracting hepatitis. I did this immediately upon returning home.

The day following my appointment with the doctor, two days after the hospital visit, I received a phone call from my gynecologist saying that my annual Pap smear had returned as class 3 (pre-cancer), and that I needed surgery within the month to remove the abnormal cells. Never had I received a Pap smear result other than class 1 (normal).

Interestingly enough, upon hearing the news from my gynecologist, I went into a state of calm. I was able to search deep within myself for the answer as to why, coincidentally or not I had created two potentially life-threatening illnesses. This to me was not a coincidence but a very big sign, a wake-up call.

I view illness as the body's way of saying to the conscious mind that something is wrong, something is out of alignment, and to look at it and try to fix it. Illness to me is like someone telling you that you have spinach stuck between your teeth and it gives you all the chances to rectify the situation if you so choose. I see illness as a second chance to get your life in order where there is chaos and disharmony.

My belief about illness is that without it, you would not know that you have driven off-course. Illness gives you guideposts as to how far off-course you are. Illness gives you an opportunity to make conscious choices to get back on track.

So, I say to you, don't see illness as an enemy: see it as your body's way of communicating with you. My body was telling me I was in great pain, physically and emotionally, yet did I listen to my body? No, and that is because I had tuned out and turned off my pain centers, remember? So, how was I to see and FEEL how much pain I was in to change the scenario, if the pain receptors were defective? So, on so many levels I thank my third husband and our dysfunctional relationship for allowing me to see where I was totally out of alignment with my soul, my life's purpose, and myself.

Two days after my 18-hour prayer, meditation, and crying episode, I received a phone call from my internist telling me that I didn't have hepatitis after all. Why did I turn yellow and run such a high temperature? I asked him. Interestingly enough, he told me, he himself had misdiagnosed me and that all I had was a case of mononucleosis. I laughed and said, "Aren't I a little too old to get that?" After all, it's called the kissing disease and mostly younger people get it. His response to me was that I must have been run down and become susceptible to the virus.

Two weeks later, I returned to my gynecologist for a second Pap smear, which I convinced her to do, because I told her that I was cured and didn't want any surgical removal of anything. She pacified me and went along with the second Pap smear, yet told me not to get my hopes up; these things didn't reverse themselves. Well, sure enough, the Pap smear came back normal. She insisted that I return for a third Pap smear that would be sent to a different lab. This time she was going to swab me with vinegar and look inside with a microscope and would then perform the removal of any unhealthy cells.

I consented to return for the third Pap, yet with the stipulation that if she could not find anything under the microscope, she was not to cut anything out. She reluctantly agreed. She proceeded to tell me again not to get my hopes up for any miraculous cure; this type of condition doesn't reverse itself. I should be prepared for the surgical removal, via a loop, of the unhealthy tissue.

As you might guess, there was no unhealthy or diseased tissue found by my gynecologist via the microscope. And the third Pap smear came back normal. Was this a coincidence or a miraculous self-healing? I choose to believe and know through my experiences that nothing in life is coincidental. You have a purpose in this life and things occur to guide you along your path. There is always a reason why things happen, harsh though they may be. Your job is to be aware of your thoughts, words, and actions so you can make conscious choices. I choose to believe that I was co-creator with the Divine to facilitate my self-healing of hepatitis and pre-cancer of the uterus. You choose what you want to believe.

This has led me to reach beyond the beyond, to see that all things are possible in the realm of possibilities, and that anything you want can be created by you. I encourage and spark you to be the captain of your ship, the master of your destiny. Do your own thing with strength and conviction and be proud of who you are and what you've manifested. Be your own icon, create your own legacy, and pass your knowledge and experience on to the next generation. Be responsible and be alive. Know you can make a difference.

Chapter Ten

Manifestation:
The Good and The Bad

Manifest Responsibly

– Ten –

Manifestation:
The Good and The Bad

*L*et's review some examples of manifestation, good and bad. Let's look at how you can create your reality by your thoughts and your words.

GOOD MANIFESTATION: Often when I am in a parking lot, I will utilize the steps of manifestation in finding myself a parking place. Yes, I do vocalize my request and will invoke the assistance from the Divine. It no longer occurs to me that I may have people riding in the car. It's become routine for me to speak out loud, totally uninhibited. The answer to the question you may be asking right now about the parking space is YES!!! Yes, a parking space will appear or someone will begin to leave a parking space and yes, the parking space is usually very close to the front door of the building, if not exactly right in front.

Do I always get front-door parking? The answer to that is NO, because I often forget to use the proper steps of manifestation and forget to ASK. Have I ever not found a parking space when I've asked? The answer is a definitive NO! What I've discovered is that when you follow the steps of manifestation, you'll get what you ask for. Again I say, be careful what you ask for. I'll cover a little bit more about this in the section on bad manifestation.

Try finding yourself a front-door parking space and see what happens. It's really an easy starting place to practice your manifestation. You have nothing to lose and everything to gain, never park in the handicap parking spots. That is selfish and harmful to others who truly need the space, along with being illegal.

Take another example: Oftentimes I'll lose track of my car speed on highways and will exceed the speed limit. I'll be signaled out by the patrol car with its flashing lights, or else it will follow me or appear behind me, speeding up to my car. During these times, what happens for me is not an intentional thought to see how I can avoid getting a speeding ticket. What happens for me is that I go into this state of "being," in which I connect directly to the Divine. By being in the state of manifestation, I ask God, OUT LOUD, to please help me not get a ticket. I incorporate the steps of manifestation, which are ingrained in my being. I usually don't have to think about them consciously.

By the sheer fact of being in the divine presence, I feel a sense of peace and calm come over me, I know that I'm going to be fine, and I begin to relax. The patrol car either stops following me, passes me, or turns around. Talk about miraculous manifestation and INSTANTANEOUS results! Do I continue speeding once the patrol car is out of sight? No. I am in such a state of gratitude that the last thing on my mind is to travel fast down the highway.

Another example of instant manifestation involved my last wedding dress. I had a dress made for me by a designer in Beverly Hills. I was living in Arizona at the time and waited very patiently for its arrival. I had already traveled to California for my final fitting and only needed to receive it. It was scheduled to arrive two days before my wedding. When it didn't arrive on the scheduled day, I began to worry. I didn't panic because I felt that receiving it the day before the wedding date was sufficient time to have it ready to wear. When it didn't arrive the next morning, I began to panic. I called the designer, who told me that it had been sent and that he was going to put a trace on it. By the end of that day, no dress had arrived and the designer told me that it had been lost. No further deliveries were scheduled to arrive that day. He said that hopefully on the day of the wedding, the dress would arrive. Needless to say, I was frantic. The closest department store of any caliber was in the Phoenix/Scottsdale area, 90 minutes away.

So, frantic as I was, my fiancé and I decided to travel to Phoenix/Scottsdale, praying and hoping that I could find something decent to wear as my wedding dress. We had been traveling for about 50 minutes when my fiancé asked me a simple yet very profound question. He said, in between my sobbing, do you really want to see if we can find you a wedding dress in Phoenix/Scottsdale, or do you really want the one that has been specially made for you? I told him, of course I want the designer dress, the one made for me. So the next thing he said was, Bianca, then why don't you just ask for it to appear? He went on to remind me that I had a special gift for manifestation and why didn't I use it to manifest something that was very important to me instead of crying and being in a state of panic?

Wow! What an idea. Still, I was a little skeptical, even knowing that when all the principles are at work, miracles can happen. Mind you, I was in a very emotional and chaotic state. However, I realized, in that moment, that by focusing my full attention on getting the dress and asking God to please help deliver it to me, I would probably be married in my special wedding gown.

I was in a prayerful, meditative state when my cell phone rang. It was my sister telling me to come back home, that my dress had just that moment arrived. You be the judge and ask yourself if it was coincidence or a miraculous manifestation.

I have another wonderful example of how the steps of manifestation can and do work. I was traveling from Newark, New

Jersey, to Sedona, Arizona via Phoenix with a friend of mine who was connecting in Phoenix to Las Vegas. I had a connecting flight from Phoenix to Sedona on a six-seat prop plane, the last connection of the day. As we were approaching Phoenix, I became increasingly anxious because the plane was running quite late and I feared that I might miss my connecting flight. Once we landed in Phoenix, I called the commuter plane company to notify them that I had just arrived and asked if they could hold the plane for me. I really didn't want to have to spend the night in Phoenix. The woman stated that, due to darkness and high winds, they could only safely postpone the flight for 15 minutes, period. I said okay, I'd be there. I still needed to claim my luggage and go outside to catch the airport shuttle bus that would take me to the terminal for private planes. All this was to happen in 15 minutes.

Phoenix airport is not a small airport. Needless to say, when my friend and I arrived at the baggage claim area, the luggage belt was not moving and no luggage from my flight had been unloaded. In that moment, I remember clasping my hands together, turning my head skyward, closing my eyes and asking out loud for assistance from the Divine. I remember asking God to please bring my luggage to me quickly so I could leave and catch the bus.

In that instant, the buzzer and light went on and the conveyer belt began to move. My luggage was the first piece off the conveyer belt. I instantly thanked God, grabbed my luggage, said good-bye to my friend and was out the door. The airport shuttle bus to the terminals had just arrived as I was leaving the building and it took me straight to the appropriate terminal. Not only had the plane waited for me, the pilot had personally walked to the bus drop-off to meet me and to carry my luggage to the plane. Wow! Again I ask, was this coincidence or a miraculous manifestation? You be the judge.

By the way, my friend who had traveled with me to Arizona on her way to Las Vegas told me the next day that she had to wait almost 20 minutes for her luggage to appear on the conveyer belt. She said that it was one of the last bags to come out. We had checked in together in New Jersey and our bags were next to each other.

Last, but not least important by far, is the story of my self-healing of two potentially life-threatening diseases, which I discussed in detail in Chapter Nine. How much more proof of manifestation do you need to understand that you, too, are capable of manifesting and creating wonderful things in your life?

BAD MANIFESTATION: Now, let me give you examples of when the manifestation steps work so well that unwanted or "bad" things happen. Two weeks before my birthday, almost three years ago, I was going through an evaluation of my life. This usually happens for me right before my birthday, prompting steps like deciding to go on a diet or starting an exercise program. Somehow this birthday was different. I felt that I wasn't living up to my potential fully and was a little unclear about what to do next with my life. I went into a deep space of prayer and meditation and asked God to help me break through the blocks and limitations I had imposed on myself that were preventing me from living life fully and joyfully. I went on to say to God that I would do whatever He wanted me to do but that it had to be very clear and specific so that I would GET IT! Once this request was made and filed away, it was forgotten by my conscious mind.

Exactly six days later, I fell outside my home and broke my left ankle in three places. I had what is called a tri-malleolar fracture with a partial dislocation of the ankle. It required surgery. I needed to have a plate and five screws on the outer side of the ankle and two screws on the inner side of the ankle. I had used the word "break" in reference to wanting to rid myself of my blocks and limitations, and what I got was a broken ankle.

You get what you ask for, so be very conscious of what you are asking for and what the ramifications might be. Yes, the ankle break took me down a much different path, changed my life, and forced me into a period of quiet reflection, and yes, it forced me to ask for help.

Even much more difficult for me was to receive help. This was a period of my life where I was forced to go into my feminine/receptive mode where I depended on others to give me care in one form or another. It was a very strange and vulnerable period for me, yet one in which I learned to let go of control. I allowed myself to receive, trusting that I was going to be taken care of. It gave my older son, who temporarily moved back into my home, along with my maid, the opportunity to assume the authority role. It gave my son especially a sense of importance and responsibility. He thanked me for this opportunity to be the one who carried the responsibility of care giving and said that it was an honor to be in this role. That situation changed my life and that of those closest to me. I say, thank God for the opportunity to grow, evolve, and change. The next time I choose to evolve or change course, I'll make sure I use terms that are more in keeping with what I want to create, like joyful, loving, and effortless, rather than wanting to make a "break" with the past!

Another example of creating something that could be termed bad or negative happened during a seminar I was attending. I wanted to be left alone and wanted not to interact with others, at least for this one particular day. I went into a space where I became very serious in my request to become invisible. I felt calm, safe, and alone with no one bothering me. I didn't want to address anyone or respond to any questions and answers. I felt invisible and alone and it felt good. Then all of a sudden, a lady came close to me and began to sit down—ON MY LAP—as if I were truly invisible. When I pushed her away, before she sat on me, she exclaimed, as she turned around,

"Oh, I'm so sorry, I didn't see you." So, I say, be careful what you ask for because you'll get it.

Another more serious example entails the creating of potentially life-threatening diseases. Sometimes you believe that you don't want to live life the way it is and you'd do just about anything to not have to deal with the unpleasant and ugly things of your life. You say things to yourself and to the Universe, such as "I'd rather die than..." or "You won't catch me dead doing or being like..." or "You make me sick because..."

Be careful with what you think and what you say, consciously or otherwise, because your brain/body doesn't know you are just blurting out an emotional comment, and that you really don't mean it. Hopefully you don't mean it.

Here is another good example of how you can manifest bad or negative things or patterns in your life. Let's say you grow up in a family environment where your parents are constantly fighting verbally and there is much gossiping and backbiting between the two. When one or the other comes to you with unpleasant, ugly stories about the other, you might ask that parent why he or she puts up with it. Why doesn't he or she leave? The answer you receive might be something about marriage being for life, or because they don't believe in divorce, or something similar. In that moment you decide NEVER to stay in an unhappy, unhealthy union and you take steps to create or manifest your exit. So begins your life of revolving doors in relationships with the opposite sex.

You've decided not to live life as your parents do, so you manifest the complete opposite. You run when the going gets tough. This is also a manifestation, a negative or "bad" one that began the moment you decided not to live in an unhealthy, miserable union. Were you totally conscious of what would happen when you made this decision? Probably not. Many things unconsciously were and are probably still a determining factor in your exits from relationships that don't seem to be going your way. This is where you would need to sit down and analyze all aspects of why you think you run from intimate relationships and whether you really want to be in one.

Sometimes we think we'd like to be in a very loving, intimate relationship yet we do just about everything we can do not to attract, develop, or maintain one. There always seem to be so many excuses, such as "I'm too busy," or "It will tie me down and I can't do what I want to do." Or how about "Relationships are nothing but trouble." Fill in the blank with this one. I'm sure you can think of many more reasons why you stay away from intimate relationships.

I ask that you choose with conscious intent and plant the seed of your manifestation. You will then be able to create your true heart's desires. Your life and how it has manifested is your creation. Make it conscious, loving, fulfilling, and resplendent. Know the difference between the two—conscious vs. unconscious—and commit to your journey of majestic manifestation.

Chapter Eleven

Manifestation or Manipulation?

Use Your Power
to Manifest
not Manipulate

– Eleven –

Manifestation or Manipulation?

From the female comes all life. Through your feminine comes your ability to manifest.

Through your feminine comes your ability to manipulate, too, if you are not careful. The power begins with the feminine principle, so females hold a tremendous responsibility when it comes to guiding and influencing the men in their lives. This was something that I didn't realize until I became a mother of two boys. I grew up believing the man was stronger, superior, and made all the decisions. With a strong father and so many older brothers and male cousins, I had no other point of reference. Having given birth to my boys, I came to realize how vulnerable and fragile the male psyche is and how easily manipulated it can be, if allowed. This became even more evident during my children's high school years.

My older son was and still is what I would call Mr. Conservative, yet he came home one day from high school with his hair shaved into a Mohawk. His only explanation was that a friend at school, a girl, convinced him that he would look so much more handsome with it and shaved it for him. He later shaved it all off, yet this very strongly demonstrated to me how easily a word or desire from a female, especially a girlfriend, could make a man do something he would not do ordinarily. This is when I truly began to notice the power females have in how they speak to and influence the men in their lives. With power comes much responsibility and it should not be misused. This is where a woman, if not living in integrity, could manipulate and control her man instead of being a loving and supportive guide for him. As a mother of two sons, I pray for good women to be in their lives to help guide them in a loving and nurturing way while being a strong grounding and guiding force.

No one wants to believe that his or her desires are selfish or self-serving or might hurt someone in the process. We all have free will. It's not ethical or universally correct to willfully change or manipulate someone else's life. When someone incorporates or overrides another's will or free choice, then that person has stepped over the line of manifestation into manipulation.

Manipulation is more common than you might realize. There may be times when you find yourself doing something you really don't want to do and wonder how you got yourself into this situation. Chances are you were somehow manipulated, consciously or not; to do something someone else wanted you to do for them. Look back at the times when you awoke to a situation or life circumstance that you realized wasn't of your own choosing. You may have realized you were living someone else's life or living for someone else and that you lost your direction. You lost sight of your dreams.

What happens when you use the Eight Steps of Manifestation to manipulate someone or something that is independent of yourself? What is the dividing line between these two factors? How do you determine when it's truly manifestation or when it is manipulation?

Can you see yourself in the role of manipulator when you try to convince someone to do something for you? You may feel it's harmless, that everyone does it, so why not? Yet how does it feel when you realize that you've been manipulated, duped, or taken advantage of? Not too good, I would imagine.

With authority and power comes great responsibility. You must be extremely careful with what you are trying to manifest within your life. The spoken word is extremely powerful. As much as it can create, it can also destroy. Once I made the mistake of pointing out a truth, as I saw it, to a female friend, thinking that it was an innocuous remark, a simple fact, from my perspective. The response from her was totally shocking, so much so that the intensity of her words still chill me to the bone. With anger and extreme hurt in her voice she made me see that for as much importance as she placed on my words, while receiving guidance and inspiration, she was also being destroyed by those words, the blunt truth. So I say, you are not responsible for the way someone receives your words and your actions, yet you are responsible for any backlash that you might experience. Make a note of your verbal responsibility and what you may be creating with your spoken word.

Throughout your life you are continually creating, either through conscious or unconscious manifestation or manipulation. You manipulate when you impose your will onto someone else. You manifest when you create for yourself or with the consent of those involved.

Let's say you love someone who is in love with someone else. What do you do? Do you accept the situation as it is? Do you openly speak your truth to the one you love or do you manipulate the situation so that person will leave his or her love and come to you? Everyone knows the many ways you can manipulate a situation in your favor, yet there is always a VERY high price you pay for manipulating someone else's life.

You can change your life all you want. You can get into shape and lose weight, become more loving, or increase your circle of friends and interests. This falls into the category of free will, so it's okay. To change someone else's life is crossing the boundary from manifestation into manipulation. Now, to see someone else change because of the changes you've made within you is fine and usually happens in close relationships. This is the other person's free will and should be accepted as such. You would only hope that the changes you make within yourself are all good and positive, perpetuating more of the same in and around those you love.

You are not responsible for what others think or do, only for your thoughts and actions. Be your own creator and co-create with the Divine. Leave everyone else to do their own creating, whether or not you may think they know what's good for them. You don't know what their life lessons may be. I spent so much of my time and energy trying to help individuals take charge of their lives. I wanted them not only to feel better but also to understand and GET IT! I wanted them to get the fact that they have control over their lives. It can be frustrating to both parties when expectations are not met.

If you want to see changes in your life and your relationships, begin with yourself first. Don't obsess about whether others are doing it right or wrong. When you focus on yourself and the results you want for yourself, the chances of getting those results are much greater. Don't force others to do things or see things your way. Leave them with their own individuality and beliefs and allow them to be independent thinkers. You and they will be much happier.

Let go of others, take care of yourself, and know that with your love and guidance they can choose their life and their lessons, using their own free will. You are not being cold and selfish. You are giving them the gift of love with the knowledge that you have taught them to fish. If they get hungry enough, they will start fishing on their own. So don't worry. Have faith that you, as they, are in control of your life and can have it just the way you want.

If you manipulate others to do your will, you have disempowered them and taken away their free choice. This is an energetic imbalance. As in physics, for every action, there is an equal and opposite reaction. Don't let this rebound back to you in a negative way, which is quite possible. Let's take the woman who wants desperately to marry her boyfriend, yet he's not very interested. She convinces him that she is pregnant, and they marry. When he finds out she is not pregnant and that he was manipulated into the marriage he becomes so angry and upset that he makes her life a living hell. So, did she get her wish? Yes! Was the price she had to pay—misery and lack of love—too high? You be the judge.

Nothing in this life happens without some consequence, either positive or negative. So yes, you can manifest, through manipulation, whatever it is you want, yet know that when you begin the process of creating from a negative position, the result is usually negative and carries a hefty price tag.

Whatever it is you think, feel, and believe, is what you will create, whether it's considered good or bad. There is no distinction. Have you heard yourself or others say, "Oh, I'm so tired of..." or "I'd just die if..." or "I'm so stupid" or "I look so fat"? These are just some examples of how your thoughts and words set you up to create just that. If you were more conscious of your thoughts and words and realized that what you think and project verbally to the Universe is already on its way to being created, you would probably use more positive wording! I hope this helps you to think more consciously and responsibly before you begin your quest for creating your ideal life.

Ask yourself if you really want the desired object. Visualize yourself in the scenario of your new creation. Sense what it would feel like in this new life, and then make your conscious choices. Life is what you make of it; so don't spend too much time focusing on the negative because that is what you'll end up with. As my mother told me when I was pregnant, "Honey, think pretty thoughts, look at pretty pictures so your child will be born pretty." She would cut out pictures of beautiful babies and bring them over to my home so I could always have beautiful babies to look at. I originally laughed at what I thought were her simple-minded statements yet little did I realize how right she was. As you can probably guess yes, both of my boys were beautiful babies (truly beautiful) and are handsome young men today.

You are what you think you are. It's that simple and yet it can be that difficult to create. Why, you say? It's probably because you may be having a hard time visualizing yourself the way you want to be or having what it is you want to create. This might have something to do with feelings of self-worth or the lack thereof. Suffice it to say, if you can think and visualize yourself a certain way with specific things happening, then you can create it. It's as simple as that. As the saying goes: "If you can name it, then you can claim it." Now it's up to you—actually it's always been up to you—to begin changing your life. You may be wondering just how that is possible. My answer to you is, start with yourself first and the rest will follow.

Chapter Twelve

What Happens When You Can't Say NO

Learn to
Trust Yourself

– Twelve –

What Happens When You Can't Say NO

When people are trying to manipulate you and you are pushed into a corner with no apparent way out, what do you do? Perhaps you've been in a situation you didn't want to be in and were doing something you didn't want to be doing, yet just couldn't see yourself leaving the situation for one reason or another. Maybe it was that you felt someone else depended on you to accomplish the task, such as watering the plants or carpooling or being the speaker at a benefit luncheon. It may not exactly be a life-or-death situation, but one in which you were led to feel indispensable. Then you decided to sacrifice a part of yourself or your plans because you just couldn't say no!

Can you, right now, get in touch with that part of you that really didn't want to do something? What thoughts and feelings are coming up for you now? If they are feelings of resentment or anger or victimization, or of feeling burdened, then they are feelings that are carrying unhealthy energies that may still be within your body. These unresolved feelings transform into energetic blockages that can create deviant energy flow, which may be a precursor to disease.

You've often heard that your lifestyle can determine your well-being. If you are a smoker, you are increasing your risk of developing heart disease, cancer, or a number of other related diseases. If you are a workaholic and don't allow yourself enough physical rest or avenues to release stress, you are potentially setting yourself up for heart disease, high blood pressure, stroke, and other related diseases.

So, what makes your holding in anger or resentment any different than the above examples? Actually, I feel there is little if any difference. Anything that drains you and your energy is a potential disease or accident waiting to happen. You are increasing your risks of leading a much less healthy life. When you are in the flow of the Universe and everything about you and your life is in harmony, situations and circumstances just flow, creating multiple synchronistic events. Have you ever experienced a time when everything during a day just seemed to click, to come together effortlessly? This is what's called being in sync with the universal flow.

Let's say you are an athlete and you've been training for a special event. You are in good physical condition. You feel strong and rested on the day of the event, and you are not overly anxious about the competition. You feel that you have a great chance at winning a medal. You are positive about the entire situation.

All your senses are heightened as you approach the starting line. The gun goes off. You lunge forward into the race and you find yourself in a semi-suspended, semi-altered state where your limbs are moving effortlessly and you feel like you are flying. You feel as if there is no limit to what you can do and so you do what you do best, you RUN. You run so fast that even you are amazed at what is happening. You pass the finish line, the crowd is roaring, and you turn to see that you have broken the state record. You have just tapped into the universal flow and surfed on the wave to victory.

All people are capable of doing something of great magnitude when they tap into their inner flow and harmonize it with the universal flow. When things seem easy, smooth and effortless, that is your indication you are on the right path. When you feel difficulties, obstacles, or experience one problem after another, this is usually your indication that somewhere you are off track and it's time to slow down and reevaluate your life.

If you are asked to do something you don't want to do and you have the option to say no but don't, know that you may be setting yourself up for some future problem. You could possibly become a passive-aggressive person. You could become volcanic and eruptive, which could be an overreaction to a situation that didn't warrant it. You could stuff your emotions and overeat, become irritable, or worse yet, create some type of disease like ulcers, high blood pressure, headaches, or heart disease.

When you cannot stand up for yourself or cannot be honest with yourself and those around you, you are truly doing yourself a disservice. You are leaking precious time and energy by holding on to something that is unpleasant and unhealthy for you. Holding on to anger, frustration, guilt, or anything negative drains you of your life's essence and decreases your ability to manifest the things that you want to have in your life.

Think about all the time, energy, and power you've lost while talking or complaining of something that you could have avoided by just saying no. Think about what you could have done with all that extra time and energy to create something beautiful and fulfilling for yourself. Think of all the power you lost by not staying honest and in integrity with yourself and doing something for someone else, all the while hating them and yourself for doing it.

You're asked to head yet ANOTHER committee to raise funds for some charitable organization. You love the organization and the other volunteers, yet you've just finished a large fundraiser. You feel you need to spend more time at home with your family, who has been complaining of your many hours away from them.

You are told how invaluable you've been to the organization and that, with your leadership, the fundraisers have been an enormous success and would you PLEASE consider doing it again, just this one more time? Sound familiar? Then you hear your answer back to them, "Of course I'll help you. I'd be delighted to do so."

What is wrong with this picture? You immediately know that you've made a wrong choice. Because you feel you can't go back on your word, you just smile and walk away with a rock in your stomach and the weight of the world on your shoulders. Why, you ask yourself, did you say yes again, and why couldn't you just say no? That is the real question you should be asking yourself. Why couldn't you just be honest with everyone and say NO? No, I'm a little tired and would like to take a short break from the leadership role because I would like to take a little personal time. Or... No, not this time because my family has been mentioning that they miss seeing me at dinner. Whatever the truth is for you is what you should have said.

No one can deny you your truth. They may not like it but it's your truth, your foundation, and when your foundation is strong and solid, no one can manipulate you into doing something you don't want to do.

Let's go back to the scenario of heading a fundraising committee. You go home feeling burdened and mention it to your family. They react by saying, "Oh no, not again." Then you get defensive and explain to them why you accepted this duty, all the while wishing you hadn't. You have now lost even more precious time and energy that could have been used to do something satisfying and healthy for yourself.

This might lead to resentment toward the organization for wanting and needing you so much, and toward your family members, who generally might try to make you feel guilty for deserting them. Worse yet, you then begin the process of self-deprecation for being such a pushover and feeling that you are weak and spineless because you couldn't and didn't say no. WOW! What a cycle and what a waste of time and energy. Get my drift?

What I'm trying to make absolutely clear is that you are in total control over your life. The sooner you gain this understanding, the sooner you can start living a more conscious, productive, and happy life. What would be the very worst thing that would happen to you had you said no to your friends in the volunteer organization? Would it be that they wouldn't be your friends anymore? Would it be that they would talk about you behind your back and think ill of you? Would they kick you out of the organization? The answer to all these questions is a no, and would you then no longer feel invaluable or indispensable? Possibly. Maybe this is what you need to look at, not the organization or those in your family who seem to put demands on you.

Maybe you just can't say no at times when you really want to because you have the need to be loved and accepted. Often you may find yourself just doing and being a certain way because it's the accepted way, yet it does nothing to lift up your soul or to bring more love and divine light into your world. What it does do for you is allow you a place of acceptance within your community, giving you a sense of belonging. This is not unique to you. It affects most humans and animals alike.

There is nothing wrong with wanting to belong, to be a part of the group. But when the group dictates who you are supposed to be, this can create great problems for you. By this I mean you may allow yourself to become a clone of others in authority and disallow yourself the right to be your own person with independent thoughts. There are wonderful guidelines to follow to function well within your society—laws of morality, law of human rights, for example—and yet you still need your freedom and personal choice to be able to say yes and no at will.

The more honest you are with yourself, the more authentic you can be, and the happier, more successful, and more powerful manifester you can become. When you can be, and when you can allow yourself to be, who you really are, then the power from within you will be manifested without. Your risk of being manipulated by others or situations will become almost nil. What a concept to know that you have the power to create what you want AND you have the power to avoid the pitfalls of being manipulated by someone else's manifestation.

Losing Control and Your Ability to Manifest

See Your Inner Beauty

– Thirteen –

Losing Control and Your Ability to Manifest

When you are moving through life and seem to have lost control of it, what is really happening and what can you do about it?

Have you ever been driving down the highway and all of a sudden noticed your exit, then slammed on the brakes and swerved the car toward the exit, yet couldn't quite turn the car fast enough or slow it down enough to exit? There is a split-second when you are feeling out of control with your car and the situation. You feel that the car may turn over if you aren't careful or that someone behind you may run into you and smash your car's rear end.

What can you do when you feel you've lost control of your life or situations within your life? This is a good and solid question and one that needs some attention. Let's refer to the Serenity Prayer: "God grant me the serenity to accept the things I cannot change, courage to change the things I can, and wisdom to know the difference." The wisdom to know the difference is key to our next topic. How do you know when to act and when to let go and surrender? Often what may seem chaotic to you is simply your inner guidance trying to get your attention to make a shift. Out of chaos comes order. This is the big bang theory. Don't you think that if our earth were created from that process then possibly your life could follow suit?

Chaos in your life is like putting all the ingredients needed to bake a cake in a mixing bowl. There is no rhyme or reason as to exactly where the eggs or flour or salt or butter will fall, yet somehow when all the ingredients are put into the baking pan and baked in the oven, a most delicious cake emerges. The ingredients were blended in their own unique form and combination to create a unified liquid mass. This became the foundation for the delicious cake you then eat and enjoy.

So how does making a cake or the big bang theory relate to the Serenity Prayer? The answer is in all about knowing what you need to change or do, what you need to let go of or to surrender. The thing you change or do is the blending of your ingredients, placing the ingredients into a cake pan, preheating the oven, putting the cake pan into the oven, closing the oven door, and then waiting until the cake is done. The things that you cannot change are the way all the ingredients come together in the bowl, the amount of time it takes for the cake to bake and to rise, and the aroma of the cake as it is baking. If you can determine what you are to do in the process of creating the cake, what originally seemed like a chaotic mess now becomes a wonderfully good-tasting cake. If you had never baked before or even seen the process of making a cake, then perhaps, on some level, you may have even thought that the cake was a result of some miraculous process. How could you have guessed that such a beautiful and tasty thing came from all those different ingredients?

What I'm hoping you'll see through these analogies is that what often seems like chaos or crisis is your life showing you that something is out of alignment. If you are conscious enough to know what it is you are to change or want to change (like mixing the ingredients and putting them in the cake pan and into the oven) and allow the process to occur (bake), then you have definitely increased your chances of creating something beautiful and wonderful from the chaos.

You might be overworked, underpaid, living from paycheck to paycheck, stressed, anxious, recently divorced, or feeling like you are having a nervous breakdown. You might not be able to think or even have enough energy to laugh, much less clean the house. At that point, on some conscious or unconscious level you either let go or you give up. What happens next depends on whether you've let go or given up.

I want to make a distinction between letting go and giving up. If you decide to let go of the control during those trying times in your life, then you have made a decision to allow someone else or something else to come into your life to help you in those areas you are not able to handle. Whether you receive human or divine help, somewhere within the chaos, you made a decision, conscious or otherwise, to ask for help by letting go of control. You recognized that you weren't equipped in that moment to handle the situation.

Usually wonderful things will come into your life following the regaining of order from chaos. A different, much better life appears. Take the scenario of my former patient with Guillain-Barre: He entered the hospital and went from a point of bodily paralysis, inability to breathe without mechanical assistance, and a lack of financial cash flow to being a highly creative, successful individual who was physically sound and financially stable. He let go of control of his life rather than giving up. In letting go he received the exceptional help required for him to change his life FOREVER and for the better.

On an energetic level, giving up is the total opposite of letting go. Letting go opens the door for assistance to come into your life. Giving up completely shuts that door and doesn't allow anyone or anything to enter. Why does that happen and what determines the opening or closing of the doors? When you let go of control of bodily functions, what happens? The sphincter muscles relax and wastes leave the body. Once the bodily wastes are released, you no longer have the toxins that may be creating grave problems within your body. You are therefore allowing your body a chance to rest and heal itself and to absorb the proper vitamins and minerals required for good health.

Here's another example: Your body is in turmoil. You are tired, stressed, feeling ill, and you don't see an end to the illness or pain. You decide that you just can't continue this way, so you make a decision that it's not worth it and you give up your medical care. You stop all treatment and procedures. You close the door to any outside medical help that may aid with your healing, including your own self-healing. If you had let go of the current treatment to allow a wiser and better-equipped person or situation to take over, you would have opened the door to healing.

On the surface, giving up and letting go may appear to be the same because they have to do with stopping action. In one, giving up, you close the door and shut down all possibility of something else entering life from the outside. In the other, letting go, the door is opened for something new and better to enter. Remember who you are and what you are capable of creating. Choose the path of healing and allow the Divine within you to assist you on your journey. Be smart, be brave, and let go.

Chapter Fourteen

The Path to Communication

Follow Your Path

– Fourteen –

The Path to Communication

There are many different situations where the door can be open or shut in relation to what we want to happen or in relationships with others. Have you ever been in a situation where you were trying to communicate your feelings and point of view to someone else and that person's response to you was so unrelated to what you were saying that you started to wonder whether he or she misunderstood you, didn't hear you, or worse yet, that you were going crazy and were in some sort of time warp? It seems that you are speaking one language and someone hears you in a totally different one. This can be extremely frustrating, especially if you feel that there is a real block to communicating with this person.

If you don't have a good reason to communicate with someone—you are related to him or her, you live or work with him or her, or you are responsible for him or her—you probably wouldn't even take the time or spend the energy to translate your language into his or hers. But what happens when you NEED to communicate with someone and it just isn't happening, or the response you get is not what you want or need, or is destructive?

What happens if you seem to be hitting a brick wall or your words spill out through holes and you cannot retrieve them? What do you do if you cannot even agree with others about what was said? These are the times when the frustration becomes so great that you want to scream or pull your hair out or shake the other person. It's similar to turning on the radio to one station at a certain frequency and the other person is tuned into a totally different station at a totally different frequency. The two stations, independent of each other, are playing beautiful music, yet when they are playing together, all you can hear is static or NOISE that is rather irritating to your nervous system. Why do you think this happens? It's the law of harmonic resonance or harmonic dissonance. Either you are in unison with each other and flow in harmony, or you are not. When you are not, discordant energy occurs in one form or another.

First, ask yourself why you want to communicate a specific message to a certain individual. Is it because you need to express how you feel on a certain subject? Is it because you want to educate or help someone? Is it because you want to scold or criticize that person or feel superior? Is it because you love someone and want him or her not to suffer? Whatever the reason you may have for initiating the communication, this original intent often colors how the delivery takes place.

What is the relationship between communication and manifestation? The way we communicate our wants, needs, and desires to others is the same way we communicate our wants, needs, and desires to God, the Universe, and our inner Divinity. So, if we are to create and manifest our heart's desires, then we need to better understand the art of communication.

Communication affects all aspects of our lives. How often are we not honest and authentic with ourselves? You are on a diet because you've chosen to drop a few pounds and you say to yourself that you are committed to this task. A few days into your new diet—I like to call it a new eating regime—you are shopping and smell the aromas of baking breads, pizzas, or cookies, and you start to feel like eating. You tell yourself that one slice of pizza or just one cookie is not going to hurt you, so you go ahead and eat it. Are you being totally honest with yourself or are you rationalizing the reason you choose to eat the "forbidden food"? This is so important to recognize because if you cannot be totally honest and accountable with yourself, how do you think the universal mind, you inner guidance, will respond to your mindset? If you cannot be clear about what you want, how then will you be able to relay to the Universe in a clear and exact way what it is that you want to manifest? Being conscious of your thoughts and actions, being honest with your self-evaluations, and developing the path of good communication are all key in assisting you to manifest your heart's desires.

Let's return to the topic of crossed wires or communicating on different wavelengths. Where do you go when you have reached your level of patience with someone who doesn't understand your language? You've tried all methods of communicating (calm words and demeanor, taking deep breaths to calm and clear the mind, proper age-specific vocabulary, logical mindset, staying in the first person, using words like "I feel," staying away from accusing wording), and still nothing seems to work. What do you do?

When all else seems to fail, go to a fail-safe solution: Go into your heart, relax, and calm yourself. Let your heart speak to you and give you the answers you need to help communicate your message. When you speak or act from your heart, you will never offend, confuse, or alienate anyone. This works for me every time. It gets me off the "hamster's wheel" and into my deepest well of inner knowing and heartfelt love.

If what you truly want to accomplish is to communicate your message and you are in your heart, the other person will be able to receive the message, no matter what the content, without taking offense or becoming angry. If what you really want to communicate is something that will make you seem right, or prove a point, then you are not in your heart. The response may be something that you don't want to see or hear.

Let's go back to the original question of why tuning in and communicating your thoughts to someone and being on the same wavelength can sometimes be difficult. During these situations I have learned to defer to a higher power, a higher intelligence that has access to solutions to all types of problems. Once I've reached the level of my inner guidance, I listen for alternative ways of communicating my message. Usually I'll say to myself, often out loud, "God, angels, guides, please help me to communicate my thoughts, words, and feelings to _____. Please let _____ receive it in the spirit that it was intended, and please let us not go into a place of battle."

This is a simple and direct manner for me to receive flashes of insight in communicating my thoughts. I often have to step out of the way to be able to see what can truly work in the mode of communication and to receive divine input. If the subject matter is heated, then I may be too triggered to communicate properly and may in turn communicate reactively. This only goes to fuel more of the miscommunication, because it drops me into my emotional state and I'm no longer in my heart.

Rest assured that if you are communicating at all with a disconnect from your heart, you are increasing the chances of not relaying the message in a manner that will be received by someone else, or by God, and there will be miscommunication.

Let's dissect the word miscommunication. Mis: Inability to, or being without; failure, unclear. Communication, communicate, commune: To speak, to talk, to say a few words; to convey, to connect; a community, cooperative, collective farm, kibbutz. The word alone spells out what is happening during a miscommunication. It's your inability or failure to speak, convey, connect, or cooperate within the community. Wow! So why is it you are not able to speak your thoughts in a cooperative way within the community or to a specific person? Is it because you are not thinking in the collective and instead are thinking and living only in your own world?

If you truly want to communicate and get your message across to the other side, you need to understand a little bit about the other side so you are able to formulate your message in a manner that will be received. That's because what you want to occur is to be received (the feminine receptive), so then you can relate and commune with others in life. If this were the case, then wouldn't it be advantageous for all concerned to function with the premise that everyone has his or her own agenda in this life while living in the same world?

If you were to commune and communicate with others, then it would be wise to learn the language of others so that you can connect with them. Everyone can relate to the universal feeling of being embraced in the loving arms of one's mother, grandmothers, sisters, and girlfriends—the feminine receptive. Everyone can understand that generally within the confines of these female arms, you are safe, loved, accepted, and understood. If you can see and feel how you would want to be received by someone else, why then can't you afford him or her the same courtesy? Understand that every pair of arms is as different as snowflakes or the clouds in the sky. Accept them for what they are and enjoy the blessings they can give.

Knowing and understanding that the other person is as desirous of your acceptance and embrace as you are might make it a little easier for you to accept the unpleasantness during the frustrating moments of miscommunication. Know that you are not alone in your quest for understanding. If you were more in your heart and less in your head and emotions, then there probably wouldn't be this problem in the first place. Try this special technique of communicating from your heart and see what happens. You have nothing to lose and everything to gain.

Chapter Fifteen

Walking Your Talk

Walk Your Talk

– Fifteen –

Walking Your Talk

When what you say doesn't align with what you do, what do you do about it? Haven't you heard yourself say to your children, "Don't lie, don't scream, and don't be selfish"? How many times have you outright lied, told a white lie, or had someone lie for you? For example, saying that you weren't home when the phone rang? You think it's harmless, yet what kind of example are you giving those close to you and what message are you giving yourself, God, and the Universe when you are sending out these mixed messages?

You tell your children not to make a scene or scream when they are upset and emoting and yet you yell at the checker at the supermarket because she accidentally rang up a charge incorrectly. Or... you are indignant with the waiter at a restaurant and reprimand him because he spilled your drink as he was placing it on the table, and this was after he made you wait too long for it.

What would your friends and family think if they were witness to this type behavior? They might think you are not the greatest example. If your children were old enough, they would most probably point out to you the error of your ways. More than likely, those with you will say nothing and energetically try to disappear so as not to experience the impact of your anger. What type of message are you sending?

Let's deal with the issue of selfishness. You preach sharing and unselfishness within your immediate environment, at work, at home, and in your community. You feel strongly that everyone should share the piece of the pie. Yet, on some level, you are having a difficult time giving up part of your own pie. You are really hungry and feel, because you paid for it, you don't have to share if you don't want to. Or... You are just TOO busy to share some of your valuable time with your child to explain why rainbows appear in the sky. Is this being selfish? How about the times you didn't want to share a piece of information that could help the entire organization or save time and money? You decide to keep it to yourself because it was your idea, you invention, your creativity coming to the fore and you don't feel you should just GIVE it away. Is this being selfish? Let's say you own your own business and you have very good and loyal employees. They have assisted you in creating a successful and lucrative business and you are very aware of this. In spite of this knowledge, you opt not to profit-share with your employees nor give them a well-deserved raise. No one says you must do anything, yet where is your sense of integrity and fairness? Don't you feel they deserve a larger piece of the pie? Is this being greedy and selfish?

There are so many more examples of situations where you don't walk your talk and, guess what, people do notice. The Universe, God, and your inner God-self also do notice. You may not care or may feel that you can change this pattern whenever you want. You may feel you had a good reason to do exactly what you did. You may feel it was an exception to the rule, or you're not normally like that and don't want others to start judging. Does this sound familiar at all? Deflecting the attention away from yourself gives you protection from being exposed.

If you cannot hear and see what you say and do and if you are not totally honest with yourself about it, then how can you change and improve your life to manifest what you say you really want? There is much confusion and crossed wires within your immediate world. The vehicle (your body), the command panel (your mind), and the control switch (your free will or choice) become convoluted. You are not sending the right message to the proper receiver, so it gets lost, and you've wasted precious time and energy. I'm addressing this statement to you, the one whose life may be sad and miserable, and the one who may feel unproductive and like a floater. I'm addressing you, the procrastinator, the doubter, and the one who lives in denial or in a fairy tale. I'm addressing you, the one who feels above all life's ups and downs. I'm addressing you, the one who has it all under control, who feels that you have nothing to hide and therefore nothing to improve in your life.

Yes, you are all part of life's puzzle, the human race. We are all part of this growing and ever-evolving species of individuals who want to get it right, who want to be happy, who want to be healthy, wise, wealthy, and loving.

In the end, everyone wants the same things when it's been analyzed or reduced to the least common denominator. The only difference is that you may want it in one form and someone else in another. You may want love expressed by having children, while others may want love reflected in their lives though creative expression. Joy for you may be the ability to hop, skip, and jump, and for someone else it may be the sheer pleasure of seeing someone smile. It's relative, yet the basic desires and needs are the same. In knowing this, know that the way you choose to manifest it in your life is a function of your free will. It is what makes you so delightfully different from your neighbor.

No one is excluded from inner reflection, from the self-scrutiny that is necessary to live a fully authentic and productive life. It only becomes easier when you are able to see yourself and your life with open eyes. Choose to see your reflection in the mirrors surrounding you. Choose to accept yourself the way you truly are. Be responsible for all aspects of your life. I'm not saying that you need to look at and criticize yourself and your actions. What I'm saying is to open your eyes and be willing to see EVERYTHING about you—your life, your dreams, your expectations, your disappointments, your potential, and your skills. See your reality. Be willing to accept yourself exactly as you are and then take responsibility for your life. Make responsible decisions. Don't look outside yourself for the answers, for the reasons, for the excuses. Be responsible, be consequent, be the creator of your life—consciously—and know that you do make a difference.

So now the question is: How can you accept yourself exactly the way you are and be okay with it all, especially if you do not like who you are or what you are doing? Let's take an extreme example. Let's say someone earlier in life decided that working an eight-to-five job wasn't fulfilling and, moreover, didn't pay the bills. She had children to support and was at a desperate time in her life. Instead of committing suicide, she decided to steal food for her children and herself. She hated the fact she was doing this. She was petrified each time she entered a store to steal and she developed ulcers. Soon after she decided to quit being a thief.

Still she couldn't find a decent-paying job that covered all the bills, so she then decided to sell sexual favors for money. She despised what she was doing, yet now there was money to feed and clothe her children and herself, and she no longer had ulcers. She hated that she made her body into something that was not honored. She hated that she allowed others to abuse it for money. Being raised in a religious family created much guilt in her and deep down in her soul, she never truly accepted her profession as okay. She felt that she could never accept herself the way she was. Know that until you can be TOTALLY accepting of where you are, whether you like it or not, you cannot change it.

In its own way your life may not be as desperate, yet think of where you are and what you do and don't like about it. Try to be conscious and honest with yourself in your evaluation. It's hard to accept EVERY aspect of yourself and your life, which may often lead you to choose a life of denial or escape, yet know that it's essential to your shifting and healing.

If you are not conscious of what you are doing and who you are in this exact moment, and if you are not able to accept it as fact, then you are virtually helpless to change. Acceptance doesn't mean liking or staying in the present situation. You, following your acceptance of your reality, are in a more powerful position to change it than if you hadn't accepted yourself exactly the way you are.

Let me give you another example: You may not like the fact that you smoke cigarettes, yet you deny to yourself and to others that you do smoke. When you choose to smoke, you go outside to hide it. You leave the house and go for a walk or take a drive in your car. You then spray the car with deodorizer and your mouth with a heavily scented peppermint spray to hide any traces of the cigarette and its smoke. Who are you fooling when you do this? If your desire is truly to quit smoking, then the longer you hide, lie, and live in denial (by saying "one more won't hurt me"), the longer you will continue to smoke.

If you face yourself and your life head-on, you increase the chances of changing it for the better. If you are an alcoholic and refuse to see this part of yourself, then how can you change something that, in your mind, doesn't exist? You can't. It's that simple.

Let's say that you do recognize that you have a drinking problem, yet don't know how to quit. Suppose you feel too weak to quit or are too scared to quit. What do you do? Well, let me first say congratulations. Acknowledgment of a problem is 50 percent of rectifying it. Acknowledgment allows you to see yourself in the mirror and say to yourself, yes that person IS I. I don't like what I'm seeing; yet I do admit that it is I.

Okay, good job, so now what? Well, it's like that spinach trapped between your teeth. Once you see and recognize that your teeth are dirty, you are bound to take an active role in the cleaning of your teeth. No one is saying that the cleaning has to be immediate. What I'm saying is that it's highly unlikely that you will forget about the spinach trapped between your teeth, and that probably one day you will take action to rectify it.

Let's take another look at your life concerning honesty and integrity. When you give your word, whether in business or personal relationships, is it okay to break it? That depends on what the situation is. If it is a situation that endangers your life or those that are entrusted to you, or if it is going to take you out of personal integrity, I feel it is safe to say that you have every right to break your word. Otherwise, I feel you need to follow through with your original agreement and commitment. You are as good as your words and actions and if you cannot be trusted to follow through on your word and agreements, then you will suffer eventual consequences. No one will want to work with or entrust important matters to you. I have often let go of financial gain for the sole purpose of keeping my word and yet on the other hand, I have broken marriage commitments due to the fact that my life and health were in danger. I cannot make this decision for you and know that life isn't always black and white. This is where you need to go within and follow your inner guidance.

So, don't be afraid to look at yourself honestly. Know that you don't have to remain any way that displeases you or brings you down. You have the gift of free will. Know that anything is possible in the realm of possibilities. The key lies in knowing what to do and how to do it. Go for it! You have the power to decide what you want and to do what you choose.

Chapter Sixteen

Community and Manifestation

Live in Harmony
with Others

– Sixteen –

Community and Manifestation

W hether or not you are aware of it, you are always working in some type of relationship with another part of your community. Whether it is your coworkers, your city, your family, or the cells of your body, you never function alone. It's impossible to have only one part of the whole doing all the jobs of the entire unit.

Let's take your body as an example: Have you ever thought about how the joint structures of your body operate? Do you realize that the bones of your body are held in place by the joint capsules, muscles, tendons, and ligaments, and that the joints have fluid and cartilage within them that allow smooth, cushioned movement that prevents bone rubbing on bone? The body is quite complex. I'm only discussing the joints of the body. There are also the circulatory system, the respiratory system, the nervous system, the skeletal system, the muscular system, the reproductive system, the lymphatic system, and all the subcategories within each system.

Now you can see how complex your body is and how much harmony is required for it to function properly. This harmony is obtained and maintained through communication! Without communication you would not be able to relay what's happening with one part of the body to another part of the body. Let's say you accidentally put your hand on a hot stove and burn yourself. What happens within your body that makes you take your hand off the stove? The impulse of the burning pain travels from the external skin to the nervous system. It then travels to the brain, where it registers that your body has been burned. The brain then shoots an impulse back to the area of the burn, via the nervous system, which in turn conveys to the muscular system to contract and move. This then mobilizes your joint to move via the skeletal system and the connective tissue around the joint closest to the burn. All this occurs in a split second, without conscious thought, and protects you from continuing to burn yourself. Do you think that your "community of cells" is communicating efficiently? I would say yes and I would further say that you need to give thanks that you are functioning well and that your body is alert, responsive, and living harmoniously within its community.

What happens when your cells aren't living and working in harmony and communicating within its community, your body? This usually signals disease within the body. The cells all require cooperation to function as a whole and to create those things within your life that bring you joy and your heart's desires and that maintain your equilibrium and health.

Community is community wherever you'd like to place it. The closer to home it is, the more essential that it function in unison and harmony. What happens when the cells within your body aren't working together well as a community? As I've said, disease usually sets in. Let's take your immune system. If your cells are unable to detect a foreign body entering you, then how do the leukocytes (white blood cells) know to fight off the foreign body, or disease (the enemy)? They don't, and that's why you contract the disease and get sick.

Another example of disease that occurs from within the body is called autoimmune disease. An autoimmune disease occurs when your body is unable to distinguish between its own cell within the community of your body and an outside invader, like a virus or bacteria. The body then begins to attack itself, thinking that it's fighting a disease, trying to keep you well and healthy, while all the time it's destroying parts of you. What a concept: Your body attacking itself because it doesn't know the difference between itself and something else. What do you think went wrong within your community of cells? Miscommunication. They're sending one message and receiving it in a different way.

How does an autoimmune disease reflect your outside life? In the world of spirituality and responsibility, the theory is that as above, so below and as within, so without. So, what is going on inside of you and how is it reflected to your outside? Lack of communication or improper communication is the culprit for self-attack, for lack of understanding and miscommunication, for battles and wars inside and outside of us.

As I've said, awareness and acceptance of the situation is 50 percent of the rectification. So what do you do with the other 50 percent that still needs to be rectified? Look to see where the breakdown in communication might be. Is it in the mental aspect, where you just don't understand or know what it's all about? Is it the emotional part of your being that is faulty and requires healing to reattach the proper connections that will send and receive the appropriate signals for good communication? Is it the spiritual aspect of your being that is out of alignment and needs guidance and help to connect with you inner Divinity, to God? Are you living a life that is destructive and setting you up for failure and despair? Only you can determine where your weakest link is and where the breakdown in communication may be. Be brave and go inside with your self-evaluation tools to see what's working and communicating and what's not.

How can you judge yourself and your potential for communication? Look at yourself via the mirrors that are all around you. If people are communicating well with you and you with them and your life in that arena is running smoothly, then you can almost consider it guaranteed that you are living harmoniously in this community. If, conversely, someone or something, such as physical symptoms of disease, mirrors back to you that something is wrong, then it is generally guaranteed that miscommunication within your community is prevalent. Make note that changes are in order to be able to function and live more harmoniously and in health.

How do you rectify the miscommunication? Simply ask, and be open to hear the response. Your body doesn't lie, and it reflects back to you what is really going on within your world. The truth may be a little more convoluted and subtly disguised than some coworker confronting you, to your face, about your rebellious nature.

If you are capable of listening to what your body has to say and what those within your community have to say, you then have guideposts as to what's truly happening within your world. You can make adjustments, if necessary, to change the disharmonious world created by your miscommunication.

Be open and honest in your communication with yourself. Be able to see the facts as they really are, so that you can make an educated decision. See what needs to be done within your community to actualize your heart's desires. Be gentle and kind; be sweet and loving with yourself. See if this helps you reconnect any faulty wiring to enable you to communicate effortlessly, quickly, and completely.

Chapter Seventeen

Drama and Manifestation:

Interactive vs. Reactive Roles

Interact with Not
React to Others

– Seventeen –

Drama and Manifestation:
Interactive vs. Reactive Roles

*D*o you feel that disharmony—drama—in a person's life is a normal human occurrence, or do you feel that drama is abnormal and only occurs during unusual circumstances? Can you identify someone you know who would be considered dramatic or a drama queen/king? Do you notice a pattern in the way this person interacts or reacts to events?

I am aware of drama. I lived with it and also helped create it almost every day. It was particularly evident when I was younger. To this day, on occasion, I will find myself reverting back to the childlike dramatic pattern that I was familiar with. Somehow, I was generally the one who screamed the loudest or made the most noise—and I was the one generally being disciplined.

I remember once visiting my grandmother's home and playing with some of my older male cousins who were also visiting. Two of these cousins decided they wanted to tease me. Their method of teasing was to hold me down and to begin tickling me to the point where it was intolerable. I began screaming. Not being an objective observer, I'm not sure how I sounded. My grandmother interpreted the scenario, as she came frantically running outside, as being my fault and assumed that I had been the instigator of all the commotion. I was punished and brought into the house while my cousins stayed outside, playing and laughing at the fact that I was the one being punished.

Would you say that I was interacting with my cousins during play or do you think I was reacting to their teasing? I think it would be safe to say that I was reacting to their teasing and expressed myself quite dramatically.

My younger son was also prone to reacting quite dramatically in situations, especially when he was in grade school and junior high. There were several instances where I thought his life might be in danger, just by the tone of his voice. Once, I returned home from the grocery store and heard, as I opened the back door, a blood-chilling scream from my younger son and thought that his older brother was killing him. I dropped the groceries I was carrying and ran to the bedroom to find my older son standing there, laughing and looking at his younger brother making these horrific sounds. They had gotten into an argument and my older son had pinched him. This precipitated the horrendous sound from my younger son. Did he dramatically overreact to the situation? I would have to say yes.

Why is it that some people are so much more dramatically expressive than others? It could be simply that they are uninhibited where emotions are concerned. It could be their passionate tendency to express themselves with their arms, facial expressions, and body language and, when excited, to elevate their voice and the energy behind the voice. It could also be that they need to make a point while being the center of attention. Maybe it's because they have a short fuse and are not disciplined enough or controlled enough to monitor the explosive feelings. Whatever the reasons for the drama, know that it's a heightened expenditure of energy, energy that could have been used and channeled to manifest some wonderful things within their life. This energy could have also been used to maintain a healthy body, mind, and spirit.

Behavior like this in human beings is usually described as animalistic or as reactive, coming from the reptilian brain. My father (now deceased) was a loving and VERY passionate man who was extremely demonstrative and would let you know, in no uncertain terms, what he was feeling. In looking back, I'd have to say that my father lived in one big drama day after day. If it wasn't one thing it was another. He might throw a plate of food across the table because his eggs were cold, or slam the door shut SO hard that the walls would rattle, or kick his heel into the wall and create a hole. Were these necessary demonstrations or expressions of emotion to get the message of discontent across? I don't think so. Would you then classify these acts as dramatic and reactive events? Most probably yes. During these moments of reaction, my father was probably operating from his hindbrain or reptilian brain and not from a centered, loving, and controlled space.

Have you ever experienced this type of drama and later, upon review, asked yourself, "Where did that come from?" As atypical as you would think acts like my father's were, they are more common than you might realize. If you were raised in a dramatic, reactive environment, chances are that you carry remnants of this drama. It's possible you have become so overly desensitized to this type of behavior that you may not even realize that you are experiencing it.

Let's look at another example of a potentially reactive situation: You are standing in line to buy a ticket at a movie theater and someone, in a bad mood and in a hurry, rushes into the line, attempts to walk past you, and physically bumps you very hard. What is your first reaction? You want to push back, right? That's a normal response, to push back when pushed, especially if pushed aggressively. Let's say your instinct is to push back, yet you choose not to. Instead you either vocalize your feelings or you say and do nothing. Your conscious awareness gives you free will to choose to respond or not, which would be an interactive rather than a reactive mode. Many an argument and physical fight have been started from someone pushing the other's buttons, whether consciously or not, which then creates a reactive response.

When something is said or done that pushes your buttons and may set you into reactive mode, what is this telling you? More often than not, it's saying that there is an unresolved issue that has been touched, creating a knee-jerk response. Your exact response usually indicates just how unresolved that issue is. The stronger the reactive response and the greater the number of buttons pushed, the more you are affected by what has been done. It could be that you have suppressed an issue so deeply, like a splinter buried under the skin, that it doesn't come up to the surface to make itself known until some outside person or force pushes those buttons. Putting pressure on the splintered area brings back some stored memory of pain, which causes you then to react.

In college, I perceived myself as being a good student who made good grades and was always prepared for class. One day I went into class unprepared (I had partied the night before), and the professor announced a pop quiz. I was mortified because the night before I had failed to review my notes. This was out of character for me, partying or not. I instantly went into reaction and began to panic. I told the professor that I was probably going to fail the quiz because I was unprepared. After my dramatic scene he assured me that I would do fine. I was a good student and had no need to worry. He was right. I made an A on the exam.

Why do you think I overreacted to his announcing a pop quiz? Could it be that I always wanted to be the best? Was I afraid of failure, or was it that I didn't want to lose face with the professor and my peers? Or was it simply that I feared being out of control in this situation? It's amazing to notice how easily I was knocked off balance by two words: pop quiz. That tells me that I wasn't centered. I wasn't connected to my inner guidance.

Have you ever been rattled while driving in traffic, when someone repeatedly and aggressively honked his horn at you while making rude gestures? This has happened to me more than once—one time especially, which I'll never forget. It was a time when I almost had an accident with my children in the car. They were young and strapped into the backseat with their seat belts. I was driving down a busy street. I was feeling some tension because of the traffic, and from my two boys, who were misbehaving. I started to reprimand them when the driver behind me began honking, indicating that I should either speed up or move out of the lane. My first physical reaction was to speed up, then move to the other lane. As I did so I felt the tension increase. Out of my reaction and my desire to get the person to stop honking the horn, I almost caused an accident. Thank God, nothing happened and no one was hurt, yet this experience taught me a great lesson.

I learned that no matter what is happening outside and around me, I must hold my center, my position. When I let emotional drama take over, I am giving up total control of the situation. The realization that my reaction could have endangered my children was a scary thought and it definitely opened my eyes to the difference between appropriate behavior and reactive drama. I allowed a total stranger to dictate my behavior because I allowed myself to get off my center, be uprooted, and go into reaction.

A tool to help you in a situation like this is consciousness and centeredness. The more conscious you are, the more capable you can be with your manifestation skills, the more you will be able to bring into your life what you really want. When I now hear cars honking at me or around me, I look to see if my speed is okay and whether I'm in the proper lane. If all checks out, I take a deep breath and assure myself that I don't have to do anything to please the other driver. I choose to stay centered and calm. This is SO essential in maintaining balance and safety in life.

So, button pushing doesn't mean you have to react negatively. When you have your buttons pushed, look at the "why" of the situation, and choose not to respond. You don't even have to evaluate why your buttons have been pushed. Just noticing that you have a charge on an issue is enough intelligent synthesis to allow you free choice not to react. You don't have to go into a reactive mode at all.

Reaction or the reactive mode is human, yet very unconscious. That's because it's from the primitive, reptilian brain. It's the undeveloped brain that reacts, usually from fear, and doesn't think first. That doesn't mean you cannot or won't respond. Responding to a stimulus is natural. You can choose the response that is appropriate for you.

What is it that might compel you to go into drama or overemphasize the situation at hand? Let's say you are fishing. You're not having much luck, yet finally you feel something tugging on your line. You reel it into the boat and see that it barely falls under the category of a "keeper," so you toss it back into the water. When relating the story to a friend, you mention just how BIG the fish was and how it got away. Is this truth, exaggeration, or drama? You be the judge.

Why is drama created in the first place? For some it can act, consciously or not, like fuel injection, nourishment, or entertainment. Take my older son, for example. I often felt that some of the arguments and outbursts instigated by him in our home environment were for the sole purpose of letting off steam and recharging his batteries. It appeared that he got much more out of the disagreements than just emoting. He seemed to relish the arguing and would look for things to disagree or argue about. It appeared he was fully charged and was enlivened by the energy expended, whereas I, on the other hand, felt totally drained. I often wondered if he were bored and just wanted some type of interaction, so he chose a good argument to pep him up. This might probably sound odd to you, yet it was what I observed and often felt to be my reality.

It seemed as if he couldn't get enough of this type of interaction. He would complain that no one understood him. Was he aware of his role in the drama? Possibly, yet it would be safe to say that from his perspective, I was the one creating all the disagreements and drama. He would be partly right because when there is action, reaction, and more reaction, both parties are reacting within the drama cycle. All I can say is, what a waste of precious energy, energy that is your equity in actualizing your dreams, goals, and desires.

It's possible you may not know that you are living within a drama cycle because it's ingrained as your way of life. It may be the way you function. It may be the way you cope, the way you get your fuel injection, your way of being. You may not even know how to live without drama in your life. Chances are you do notice the energy drain, or feel a weakening in your immune system that might create an overall feeling of malaise. You can't quite put your finger on it but you know you don't feel 100 percent. These can all be symptoms of energy leaks through unnecessary and possibly unconscious dramatic reactions.

Think of each time your body goes into "attention" mode for fight or flight, thinking that there is danger. Your buttons have been pushed and you are on alert. Can you imagine what might be required of the body to maintain this mode? Here's an example: You are a swimmer and you've just mounted the racing block in your lane. You hear "swimmers, on your mark." You assume your position and begin to prepare mentally and physically for the dive. You then hear "get set," so now your body is on high alert. You hold this position of heightened intensity, with your muscles tense, your heart beating fast, your breathing accelerated, all in preparation for the dive into the water to begin your race. But suppose nothing happens? No one says GO. What would happen to your body if you were to maintain this state of readiness for any extended period of time? Your body would fatigue and would burn itself out.

You are only capable of holding this position of heightened intensity and stress for short periods of time before the body breaks down. The reactive explosion of the drama is equal to the swimmer diving into the water and to the pressure valve releasing pressure from the cooker. These are all acts of drama that release the built-up or stored pressure/tension that creates a space to calm down. Have you ever felt like you've just run a marathon following a heated argument? Your body thinks it has! You are putting a tremendous stress on your body.

When you go into a state of drama, often your body goes into heightened alert. The adrenaline begins pumping and you feel a high—destructive in nature, yet still a high. Some may thrive on this type of drama. For that very reason, the adrenaline makes you feel alive, even though it's in an unhealthy way. Often the way you act or react throughout life will determine the state of your health. While it may seem that negative attention is better than no attention at all, I'm here to say that the attention drawn from drama is generally unhealthy and destructive.

How do you get out of the drama cycle? The number one thing is to put it in your conscious awareness. Recognize that this may be operating in your life. Know that if you can see it in one area, such as relationships, then chances are it is operating in other areas of your life.

Second, make a conscious choice to change this pattern within your life and do proactive things that will help you change. One thing that you can do is ask your friends and loved ones to point out to you the moments when you drop into the drama queen/king mode. Try to create a safe environment where there is no blame, no right or wrong, only awareness brought to situations that you might want to change. Conversely, you can do the same for your loved ones.

Third, self-evaluate and digest. Ask yourself if your reaction to a present situation was appropriate or if it was an exaggerated response. If it was exaggerated, ask yourself why. Was it because there was some truth to what was being said and you didn't want others to know this as your truth? Was it because it made you feel vulnerable and you were having a difficult time with this? Was it because you have been in denial of your truth and you don't want to hear it from someone else? Whatever the reason, it's yours alone and only you can determine the true reasons for your actions.

Let's take a look at other possibilities behind the need for drama. Perhaps you want to be the center of attention, or you feel people will listen to you only when you turn up the juice and overreact. Is it that you feel justified and need to express it vehemently or are you wanting to hurt someone? Maybe it's because drama has always worked for you in the past so you feel that you don't want or have to change. You get what you want from others this way. Maybe it makes you feel alive or makes you feel powerful. Whatever the reason drama may be present in your life, try to isolate it as best you can, then bring awareness to the situation to help determine if this is how you want to function and live your life.

Imagine all the time and energy you use during a dramatic outburst. Let's say you are a helium balloon. Every time you overreact and dramatize a situation, you pierce the balloon with a pin, creating a small and very slow air leak. The more often dramatic reaction occurs, the more punctures you'll have in your balloon. Soon your balloon has no more air, becomes flat, and falls. This is what generally happens to your energy system, and your body.

As I've aged, I've noticed this fact to be so true for me. I can no longer rebound as quickly as when I was younger, following one of these dramatic, reactive outbursts. It can really take its toll on my body. My older son and I would have these horrific, dramatic arguments that would leave me feeling so weak and exhausted I would have to ask him to leave the room or leave the room myself for fear that my body wouldn't be able to hold up. The energy expelled during one of these dramatic situations was so intense on both our parts and so destructive that it's a wonder we are still healthy.

When these outbursts would occur, I soon realized that my body could not sustain that level of drama and I would need to find a different mode of communication, one in which my buttons wouldn't be pushed. Or in which I wouldn't react when my son attempted to push my buttons. This was not an easy task; yet it was essential for the well-being of our relationship and for our physical and emotional health, mainly mine.

At some point you will need to make choices that benefit you. These choices may not be pleasant for others. Refuse to communicate with someone for a designated period until the mode of communication is healthier from all parties involved. If you fall into the category of the one who loves a good argument or the one who loves the battle of words and the turmoil that arises from it all, think of the disharmony created within your body and your life with your words and reactions. Ask yourself if this is REALLY what you want to create.

Words are so powerful. They can be used to heal or to destroy. Be aware of the tremendous responsibility of what is conveyed to you and to others. Words can't be swallowed or erased once you've spoken them. As much as you may say that you really didn't mean what you said, that it was a mistake or a joke or you were just playing around, the reality is that the words have been released out into the Universe.

The spoken word is one of the steps of your manifestation, whether conscious or not. What you speak you can manifest, so I say to you again, be careful what you speak, because what you speak you will create. You are that powerful. If what you want is drama in your life, then that is what you will create. Look at your life, your relationships, your career, your wealth, your health, and your joy. See just what you have been doing, consciously or unconsciously, that helped create it.

If you are truly content with how your life is going and you feel that you've evolved to the point where you are totally content with all aspects of your life, then it seems you've mastered your relationship with your God-self, the Universe, God. I commend you and bless you and your journey to this point. I ask that you share your wisdom and knowledge with others who may still be struggling on their path. You, too, have a responsibility to this world that you are a part of. Assist those of us still journeying and who want to learn more as we evolve to a higher state of being. Teach us to become beacons of light that shine out to those searching for the truth, searching for light and love.

Chapter Eighteen

Love, an Open Heart, and Your Ability to Manifest

Keep Your Heart
Open to Love

– Eighteen –

Love, an Open Heart, and Your Ability to Manifest

Whereas your brain is the control panel of the body, issuing commands to the different systems of your body, your heart is the pump that supplies the force, via the circulatory system, to supply oxygen and messages to various parts of the body. The brain is key to the survival of your body. The human heart is defined as the center of emotional life, where the deepest and most sincere feelings, such as affection, warmth, and admiration, are located. It is also the place where an individual is most vulnerable to pain.

Manifestation does require that you open your heart to allow the flow of energy, your intent, and your desires, from your heart out into the Universe. An open heart is also required for you to receive what you have asked to manifest.

It is safe to say that, on some level, you love the object or situation that you want to create. Love carries the strongest vibration of emotion that can cause manifestation and create miracles. Look at all the miraculous situations that have stemmed from the emotion of love. Here are some examples: the animal who unconditionally loves his master and won't leave his side when injured; the dog who runs into a street, endangering its life, to rescue a child from being hit by a car; a mother giving her infant her food so the child can survive; or the father who gives his life for the safety of his family.

All of these are examples of love given from an open heart, whether human or animal. Do you think that if the father had a closed heart and didn't hold love in his heart for his family, he would even consider defending them and giving up his life for them? Most likely not. If his heart had been closed, he might have gone into his left brain to analyze the situation and decide whether he would endanger his life for his family. If your toddler left your side and ran into the street and into the path of a speeding car, do you think you would stop to analyze whether you should try to save your child? Chances are that you would do whatever necessary to keep your child safe because of the deep love you have for your child.

Do you need to be in an intimate relationship with someone to interact with them openheartedly? No. Let's imagine that you are on a commuter train carrying your purse, computer, and various written materials that you need to review before work. You comfortably settle into a seat, open your computer, and begin working. As you arrive at the second stop, you notice an elderly gentleman with a cane getting on. All seats are taken and he is forced to stand and hold on. Your heart goes out to him and you decide to give him your seat, although you have material still to look through. He accepts with such appreciation that it brings warmth to your heart. I would say that your heart was open to giving and receiving love. This example shows that you don't have to be intimate with or even know someone to relate to them with an open, loving heart.

This is where I feel you can truly help make a difference within your world. The more your heart remains open to give lovingly, the larger your capacity to give AND receive love. This is when blessings occur. It's similar to the old saying, "what goes around, comes around." I'm not saying that you should keep your heart open, loving, and giving for the sole purpose of receiving. What I'm saying is that when you give with an open heart, the love and light from your center radiates to others like the rays of the sun. It magnifies and multiplies and will soon return to you in grander form.

The sun shines over the earth, reaching each person, giving them all the opportunity to receive the warmth and spread the warmth to others. Don't you usually feel better on mild, sunny days and notice that your disposition improves when the sun is out? This is especially true following cold or cloudy days. I remember that during my high school years, the springtime held such a wonderful place in my heart. That was because the sun was shining more and the air was warming more and I felt more alive and ready to bloom. I usually had what people would call "spring fever." I loved the spring and still do.

How much more energy or effort would you have to expend to be openhearted and loving to someone else? Actually, the way I see it is, not any more than normal, and you are the one most benefiting from your open heart. Others around you are feeling the effects or reflections of love from your open heart while you are "being" your open heart and depositing the love and light back into yourself. The more you open your heart to love others, the more you love yourself.

Why would a person be afraid to open his or her heart to love? There are people in this world who have chosen to close their hearts and live like this day after day. Chances are you've interacted with them periodically throughout your life.

The one thing that may be happening to the individual is his or her lack of preparedness for love. His or her not knowing what to do with the love could create the scenario of the heart staying closed down. The more closed the heart, the more prone to fear a person can become. This then begins a cycle of the heart shutting down, fear creeping in, and the heart shutting down more, and even more fear creeping in. Maybe you are concerned that if your heart is open, you are setting yourself up to be taken advantage of, or that you are a prime target for harm. If this is true for you, then it's understandable that you may choose to close your heart. Know that you are the one who will suffer from the lack of love.

Let's take another example and see life through the eyes of an innocent child. This child is openhearted and loving and appears to be a blessed child. The child is so unconditionally loving and accepting of everyone and everything. There are no questions asked or stipulations made by the child, only open LOVE flowing from the heart. What happens when you see a child like this beaming and smiling at you? You smile back, right? Well, that's what sharing your light and love is all about. Sharing your light and love can be a simple smile, a handshake, a pat on the back, the opening of a door, or the giving up of your seat or your place in line to someone else. All of these acts constitute acts of love.

Like attracts like. If you are innocently pure and loving, then you will attract love and innocence and purity into your life. There is one exception to the rule and that is the role that is played by the deviants of society who follow no rules.

What I'm saying is that you will attract to you what it is that you are. If you have loving feelings in your heart, then loving people and situations will enter your life. If you generate love and warmth from inside you and radiate it out to others, you increase the chances of receiving back what it is that you generate. Imagine your heart having doors, like your home. The wider the doors are open, the more you can bring into your home, and the more you can flow out. The same applies with your heart. The more your heart is open, the more you can give and receive, and the greater capacity there is for love.

Love is defined as an intense feeling of tender affection and compassion, a passionate feeling of romantic desire and sexual attraction. It's an overused word and yet is a word that says it all. As the saying goes, "everyone loves a lover." Why do you think this is so? I feel it's because people experience love by the simple act of watching others in love. You can feel it and see it in their eyes and by the look on their faces. You can hear it in the tone of their voices. You generally come away feeling very warm and loving.

Love is contagious and yet there are still so many lacking the experience of love. When you see someone smile, it makes you want to smile. Laughing is also contagious. Upon hearing it, you want to laugh. I remember hearing a commercial on the radio— I forget what was being advertised—that featured children laughing and, no matter what mood I was in, I would also laugh. It touched my heart so deeply. The laughter was more than contagious, it was compelling, because somewhere in the process of hearing the laughter, my heart opened wider and I melted into it.

You don't have to be at a party, drinking, or at a comedy club to start your laughter. It's all around you. All you need to do is open your eyes to the magnificence of this life you are living, then open your heart to receive it all. Complete abundance is there for you to have, relish, and share.

Don't be afraid to open yourself to love and to be loved. Love is essential for your survival in this world. You often take a risk when you open your heart to love. Even so, without risk, calculated risk, there is no growth. The higher the risk, the greater the responsibility assumed, the greater the reward. From my experience, the rewards have been great when I've chosen to live with an open, loving heart.

Imagine yourself manifesting your heart's desires quickly and without effort. Imagine yourself opening the doors to your heart as wide as possible, so that you can view and understand what your heart truly wants to manifest within your life.

Why live life with your doors half-closed? Why not open your doors wide? Take the chance and live life fully, with a completely open heart and with the knowledge that you have the inner power and strength to deal with anything life brings your way. I pray you won't be apprehensive about the process of opening your heart and that you view it as an adventure above any other adventure you've ever experienced. Try to view your heart opening as the passageway to manifesting your heart's desires.

Chapter Nineteen

Tolerance, Acceptance, and Your Ability to Manifest

Be Tolerant

– Nineteen –

Tolerance, Acceptance, and Your Ability to Manifest

*H*ow do tolerance and acceptance relate to your ability to manifest? Before you can change something or yourself to be the way you desire, via manifesting, you first need to recognize and accept "what is" in the present moment. You may not like "what is," yet tolerating it is so important for you to manifest what you truly want. The more you deny or reject who you are or what you are doing, the longer it's going to take for you to change. If you are unable to accept yourself or tolerate aspects of yourself, then how can you see yourself loving that part of you that needs transformation or change?

Let's say you are teaching your children how to play tennis and they are having a difficult time keeping the ball on the court and in motion. It seems that most of your time is spent chasing balls. Are you going to be intolerant of your children's inability to play tennis or are you going to open your heart to be more loving and understanding of their situation? Granted, you realize that in time they will improve and may eventually become better players than you. In the moment you also realize that what your children need the most from you is love, tolerance, acceptance, and encouragement to help them make the shift to becoming better tennis players.

This principle of tolerance, acceptance, and encouragement applies to you, too. You need all these things, plus love, from yourself and for yourself to make it to the next level of manifestation.

This is not about being right or wrong or making good or bad decisions. It's about knowing how you perceive yourself and your life. If you feel that something is not okay within your life and you don't befriend whatever it is so that you can understand it and prepare it for change, you may end up rejecting it and trying to repel it from your life. This often creates the opposite of what you want. The more thought, energy, and focus you give an issue, the stronger a force it becomes. Instead of disappearing from your life it usually becomes larger and more present.

Let's say your child is seeking attention from you and deeply wants to be loved and accepted by you, yet doesn't quite know how to fulfill this need. He or she doesn't really want to accept the fact that he or she wants and needs your love and acceptance. Instead of approaching you with a loving, open heart, giving you love and creating an avenue to receive love, he or she approaches you with anger, silence, or neutrality, being uncomfortable with this need. What usually happens next is some form of disharmony, often resulting in argument.

How many times have you witnessed a couple injure each other through their words and actions, pushing each other farther away, when all they really wanted was to love and be loved by their partner? You see this in people, especially children, all the time. It's the need to be loved and accepted by your peers. One of two things usually happens: You conform to the group and become like them, enabling you to receive love and acceptance, or you rebel against the group, while still yearning for love and acceptance. Rebelling against the object of your desires is generally not the way to acquire it.

Try to look deep within yourself. See what it is that you may not be accepting or tolerating within your world that may be preventing you from fulfilling your heart's desires. Could it be the fear of actually attaining or being what it is you truly want? Is it a concern that your life will change and you won't know how to function in your new world? Are you afraid of the unknown? Whatever is preventing you from being or acquiring what you want from life, there usually is an underlying factor of non-acceptance or intolerance of something within yourself or your life.

If you feel the reasons for not being or acquiring what you want lie within some other person or situation, you are sadly mistaken. Nothing exists outside of you that is not already a part of you. If you believe that the sky is blue, then for you it's blue regardless of the reality. This is your belief and you cannot see differently.

Documented cases of people with schizophrenia show how a belief can actually change physical characteristics such as hair color, eye color, or bodily scarring. This often occurs when a schizophrenic person changes from one personality to another. He believes, 100 percent that he is a specific person with specific characteristics, and that is what his reality creates. As mentioned in Chapter Three, cellular biologist Bruce Lipton, Ph.D. says that an outside influence or stimulus, such as environment and your beliefs, is what determines the changes within your genetics, with your beliefs being the strongest influence.

Now knowing that your environment and especially your beliefs are what help manifest your reality, and if you believe that a certain body part is ugly and unacceptable, guess what will happen? Yes, that's right. Chances are that whatever it is you are rejecting will become larger instead of disappear.

Let's say you have decided you want to lose weight, and you begin a diet and exercise program. You start by weighing your-self and taking a very good look at your whole body in the mirror. You start eating all the right things and slowly start the exercise program, thinking and hoping that this time you are going to succeed and keep the weight off permanently. You weigh yourself a few days later and find that you've gained half a pound and you become very frustrated and disappointed. You look at yourself in the mirror and think that maybe the scale is right and you are a little heavier around the middle. This then begins a cycle of trying to cut more calories to lose more weight, and you walk an extra 15 minutes that day. Two days later you get on the scale, and there's no difference. You weigh exactly the same. You wonder how this can be and become discouraged once again. You look in the mirror and you swear that you are growing by the hour.

What's happening? Why aren't you losing weight? You're doing everything right, even more than you need to, and it's still not helping. Has your metabolism slowed down? Are you destined to be overweight just because you are getting a little older? All these questions enter your mind and you start becoming even more discouraged. You are no longer motivated to diet or exercise and in less than a week, you've given up, yet again.

I can't tell you how many times this has happened to me. It's as if I believe the scale more than my own inner guidance, and somehow I allow the scale to determine how I'm going to feel that day. I intellectually know about the concept of fluid retention and increased muscle mass, which add weight, and yet somehow I allow a machine to dictate how I perceive myself.

It all goes back to focus, desire, intent, and lack of acceptance. When you focus too much on the scale and on an imagined inch gained, rather than the progress of your exercise and diet, you allow yourself to be affected by what the scale says. You develop a lack of acceptance of yourself and your body. Somehow, you find yourself having difficulty accepting your inability to lose weight and so you create more of what it is you want to change, your weight.

If you can accept yourself exactly where you are, the way you are, you will increase your chance of success. This may sound easy to do yet I know it may not be so easy to change the way you perceive and relate to yourself.

Do you have someone in your life that confirms to you your need to lose weight? Does that person send the message that it's not acceptable to be overweight? This could be a real problem, especially in the early stages of your transformation and manifestation. Often you can attract people and situations that reflect what it is you think, feel, or believe to be true. If you truly believe that you are not beautiful, then it's relatively safe to say that the people in your life will reflect, in some fashion or other, what you feel to be true. Conversely, when you change the way you feel and what you believe about yourself, then you can also attract others who will confirm your changed perception. If you feel pretty, you will exude beauty and people will see and feel it.

Visualizing yourself the way you want to be is a strong element in its actualization. Thinking and visualizing yourself in a negative scenario can also create or amplify those qualities for you. Whatever you believe to be true will be true for you. Whatever it is that you are having difficulty accepting and tolerating will be difficult to change or transform. Would your children grow and prosper with negative and unloving thoughts and actions? I don't think so.

The more we lovingly care for what we want, the faster and greater the chance we will have of creating what we've nurtured and desired. The more we tolerate and accept what it is we want to change, the quicker it will manifest. Try not to be so critical of the imperfections within you. Know that when you can accept those small or large imperfections, this will help you learn to tolerate and accept the imperfections in others. You are here to interact with others who are not perfect. In doing so you need to have a better understanding and acceptance of yourself and others.

You don't have to like what you have problems accepting, yet if you can accept something for what it is, you can continue to relate authentically to others and yourself. Rejecting others, or parts of yourself, breaks communication. This is probably not what you really want to create within your life. Keeping an open heart can help give you an avenue by which you can experience more tolerance and acceptance. This increases your chances of consciously and quickly manifesting what you really want from life.

Be your own best friend and confidante by being gentle with yourself. Learn to be more accepting and tolerant of yourself. In loving, tolerating, and accepting who and what you are, you are reflecting to yourself and others a powerful way to change your life and to manifest your heart's desires. Trust yourself, open your heart, and begin to accept the Divine within all.

Chapter Twenty

Fear, the Shadow Self, and Your Ability to Manifest

Transform Your
Shadow Self

– Twenty –

Fear, the Shadow Self, and Your Ability to Manifest

*H*ave you ever been in a situation where you have been frightened or apprehensive and couldn't think or act intelligently or rationally? Have you ever had to remember an infrequently used phone number during an emergency and your brain couldn't retrieve it? Have you ever been with a person having a heart attack or in need of emergency help and didn't know what to do, and did nothing? Have you ever failed at something—an exam, a job interview, a business, a relationship —and didn't know where to turn?

These are examples of situations that carry a potential for experiencing fear. If you haven't experienced these specific situations, possibly you've experienced something similar that had you feeling fear of some sort. After the experience, did you say to yourself, why didn't I do that, or why couldn't I remember? If you've answered yes, then you were probably functioning outside of your heart.

"Where there is love, there is no fear" (New Testament: 1 John, Chapter 4, verse 17). The law of physics states that two things cannot occupy the same space at the same time. If you are in love, you cannot be in fear, and if you are in fear, then most definitely you cannot be in love and in your heart. It's impossible.

Let's look at a physical example of two things trying to be in one place at the same time. You are getting ready to dive into a swimming pool. You notice the level of the water in relationship to the tiles on the inside of the pool, and then decide to dive in. What happens next? The water is displaced in direct proportion to your body weight and force of entry. Your body replaces part of the space within the pool by displacing some of its water.

Where there is fear, love cannot exist. If you are in fear, then your heart is probably shut down. You then may go into panic mode, disconnect from your inner guidance, and are no longer in your heart, connected to love. If you are no longer in love, then you are operating from a different point of reference. While experiencing fear, your mind gets messages of distress and sends fight, flight, or freeze messages to the body. Remember the swimmer on the starting block holding the position of "ready, set"? You can only hold this position for a short period of time before the body and immune system begins to break down.

Now, try to visualize yourself manifesting a sense of peace and safety when operating from a place of fear. It's very difficult, if not impossible. Better yet, try to visualize yourself manifesting your mate, your dream career, your health, your wealth, your heart's desires in this heightened state of fight, flight, or freeze. It's not very likely that you will be able to do it.

So, if your heart, mind, and soul are not in control during these fearful, stressful situations, then who or what is? Obviously something or someone is giving orders to your body and its functions and if it's not the conscious mind, loving heart, or divine soul, then who or what is it? It's similar to being on automatic pilot when something or someone else takes control and makes all the decisions. Remember, whoever is in charge is the commander of your manifestation. If you want to be conscious in your manifesting and not fall victim to your unconscious thoughts and feelings, then you should be aware of who is making the decisions. You probably are saying to yourself, "Of course, I'm in control of what I do, I make all the decisions." Yes, on some level this is correct. You are the one in your body who is acting or reacting to a situation. Yes, you are the one mentally sending signals throughout your body, telling it what to do. Yes, you are the one who experiences the results of the decisions. BUT are your decisions made from a place of centeredness, calm, conscious thought, and full control or, when in a fearful situation, do you let your emotions take over and react instead of allowing you to act from intelligent choices?

If you were in a calm, peaceful, and loving space, you wouldn't frantically yell at your children and at the same time scold them as they run across the street. Could it be you yelling like a banshee or could it be an aspect of you, what I call your shadow self? Most probably your fear was the instigator of your reaction to their crossing the street. Do you think or feel that it was the REAL you yelling or an aspect of you doing it? I would guess that it probably was your shadow self, that part of you that lives hidden in the dark, and feeds on situations like this one.

Fear generally creates the MONSTER that takes you over and converts your actions into reactions. You often later regret any trauma you (your shadow self) may have caused. In these situations you generally are out of conscious control and out of your heart and have allowed another aspect of yourself to take over. What type of manifesting do you think this behavior would result in: peaceful, loving, trusting embraces from your child or anxious, fearful, distrusting glances?

Can you imagine yourself as the child who, innocently and unconsciously, while crossing the street, hears someone yelling and screaming with panic and terror in her voice? Do you think that this is going to show, by example, the way you deal with fearful situations? Yes, of course! He or she will probably begin reacting like you in similar situations. I can totally understand elevating your voice to call out a warning to your children so they can remain safe, yet when that call is infused with fear and terror, your loss of control mixed with panic is what is transmitted to your children. This will continue the cycle of fear while instilling greater fear in them. Your shadow self, that aspect of you that lives in the dark and thrives on fear, was probably in control as you yelled.

There are so many avenues where fear can reside that it's almost impossible to have never experienced it. There is fear of poverty, fear of loneliness, fear of failure, fear of illness, and the ultimate fear, the fear of death. When you are operating from fear, you cannot act rationally and may do or say things that, upon deeper reflection, were not coming from a place of love, light, centeredness, or peace.

Can you still manifest during a fearful situation? Yes, but I would bet it's not something that you would consciously want to have or to create in your life. Fear creates more fear and if fear is something you want to eliminate from your life, then you need to begin with your own inner fears or hidden, dark side.

Your state of mind has much to do with what you create. If you can control your emotions and attitude, then you are more likely to manifest the things that you truly want in your life. I wanted to learn to scuba-dive yet was a little apprehensive about being confined underwater at a depth that would not allow me to surface at will. I am a good, strong swimmer yet was not totally comfortable with the equipment, the techniques, or procedures of diving. Still, I decided that I was going to go out on the boat into the open sea and attempt a 40-foot open-water dive. The water was rough and choppy. The sky was clouding over and looking stormy. The boat was hitting the four- to five-foot waves and landing with a thump. All the while I was feeling that I had made a big mistake, but said nothing.

The boat anchored and the rocking began. At the same time I began feeling nauseated and attributed it to the fear of the dive.

I went into a mini-panic and announced that I was NOT going to dive, as I was feeling sick. I was assured that I would feel better once I went below the surface of the water, where the water was calmer, and not to worry any further. This did nothing to help my nausea or feelings of fear and panic. The knowledge that panicking underwater at 40 feet could result in a very dangerous situation for me didn't help relieve any of the fear or nausea.

I had a few moments to make my final decision as to whether I was going to dive or not as I gathered my equipment together (fins, mask, weight belt, vest with oxygen tank). At some point I FULLY understood and integrated the knowledge that I was in control of the entire situation. I realized that if I chose to dive to a depth of 40 feet I would be fine because my state of mind and being was in my conscious control.

The things I kept in mind during the dive were to stay calm, centered, and in my heart, and most important was not to forget to BREATHE. There were a couple of brief moments when panic wanted to creep in, yet I remained totally conscious, breathing deeply from the oxygen tank, as I had been previously instructed to keep myself calm. I reminded myself to stay centered and in my heart so the panic would be dissipated. It worked!

See how powerful you can be in creating what it is you want, especially during potentially stressful and dangerous conditions? Fear can take your power away, disabling you from functioning and acting with clarity and reason. It can reduce you to a level of animalistic reflex or unconscious reaction, while love does just the opposite. Love empowers you.

Let's now refer back to the shadow self. How was it created and why is it still in your life? Like the shade (shadow) from a tree, your shadow at times provides you with protection. It allows you to hide behind it or escape toward it, finding refuge. You may simply allow it to take the lead and make the decisions for you because you just can't or won't. It generally has a personality of its own, and on some level, you may not feel quite responsible for your actions or reactions. When the fear is too overwhelming, you may opt to allow your shadow to take over. This is often due to an inability to deal head-on with the source of fear.

The more often you choose to go into fear and go out of your heart, the more often your shadow self takes over and makes decisions that are not for anyone's highest good.

Facing your shadow self is much like walking to the edge of a cliff, looking down, and making a decision as to whether or not you feel you can jump to safety. Unless you look at fear straight on and make a conscious, openhearted, centered choice, you will continue to be controlled by your fear and your shadow self. Love radiates light, divine light, forcing you out of the shadows, and helping you to overcome your fear.

Your shadow never leaves you. It's a part of you, a part of your personality. It has often been described, in Egyptian and indigenous teachings, as the place where your soul connects with your body. It must be acknowledged, understood, and embraced to be able to be converted into love and light. You can expend much of your energy holding on to your shadow side. This is energy lost that could be used to create something you truly want.

Envision yourself gathering all the energetic force that you have used to maintain connection with your shadow self and applying this same energetic force, or fuel, to manifest the life you have always wanted. Why don't you trade the fear and terror for a new home or a new job or a new relationship, for a wonderful new and loving life? That is what you can do with all aspects of your life. Open your heart, shine the divine light into your life, infuse your shadow self with your own light, and begin the process of setting the foundation for your conscious manifestation.

You don't have to make your shadow self your enemy. Try to understand why it was created in the first place and see it as a result of your fearful self that needs education, love, understanding, and acceptance. Like the child who didn't understand the dangers of not looking to both sides before crossing the street, your shadow self needs knowledge and love, not fear and intolerance. Just as the light shining through the branches of the tree wipes away the shade (shadow), the divine light emanating from your loving, open heart will wipe away or transform your shadow self.

Don't fear your shadow self; that will only increase its strength and power over you. Love it instead. This may sound strange to you. How can you love something that is destructive, dark, and brings you misery? Once you are in your heart and experiencing love, the fear will disappear, even though the external situation that warrants a fearful reaction is still present.

Just because you think or feel you should experience fear in certain situations doesn't mean that you have to be in the fear. You have conscious choice in every situation that you encounter. Let's take the situation of a woman who was carjacked while her child was strapped into a car seat. She had the calm sense and ability to secretly dial 911 on her cell phone and, while discussing locations and directions with the hijacker, revealed to the 911 operator the exact location of her traveling car. The police eventually intercepted the car and hijacker and the mother and child were unharmed. Do you think this woman had allowed her shadow self to control the situation? I don't think she did. Somewhere, during this potentially fearful and life-threatening situation, she chose to stay calm and centered. Most probably with an open heart filled with love and desire to protect her child, she made choices that stemmed from a place of power. She manifested safety for her child and herself and the arrest of her hijacker.

"The only thing we have to fear is fear itself." President Franklin D. Roosevelt said this in his first inaugural address in 1933. This is so true. Fear is a state of mind. A potentially fearful situation doesn't mean you have to experience the fear, yet the more you feel fear, the more fear you create and the stronger your shadow self becomes. Why not reverse this destructive and unhealthy cycle and replace it with openhearted love? Love propagates more love. The more love you experience, the more peace, calm, and joy you have in your life and the more you are in control of your life. The more in control you are of your life, the greater power you have and the greater the ability to manifest your dreams and your heart's desires.

Why not choose to live your life in love, in the light, and in your power? Try not to fall victim to your fear or to your shadow self. Remember that fear is just a state of mind and you can change your mind anytime. You don't have to live a life full of fear one day longer. Choose love and see how your life can be transformed. See how much power and control you can have within your life.

Chapter Twenty-One

The Intermingling of Pleasure and Pain

Choose Pleasure
Not Pain

– Twenty-One –

The Intermingling of Pleasure and Pain

*G*ravitating to people, places, or things that give pleasure is something that often occurs unconsciously. It's human nature to want to feel good. Feeling joy and happiness is something that not only is essential for your well-being, it is what often drives your actions. The need to feel good or to feel pleasure often supersedes the method of its acquisition. How the pleasure is to be achieved is often minimized. More often than not, the end result is the primary focus, PLEASURE.

There is nothing wrong in wanting to feel good or to feel better via pleasure. If you experience pleasure and no one is harmed in the process, including yourself, then it's generally a good and wonderful experience. Often the desire to share this experience is strong. If the pleasure received is only fleeting or if the method of acquiring it is harmful to yourself or others, this usually indicates that a hefty price has been paid for the momentary feelings of pleasure.

Let's take an example, the decision to be unfaithful to your partner for the momentary sensation of physical gratification or sexual pleasure. The hefty price tag could be disease (potentially life-threatening) or the ending of your primary relationship. These factors either were not a priority in your decision-making or were outweighed by the desire to feel the pleasure. Too many of these types of decisions, geared toward self-gratification, can lead you down a path where the manifestations created are unhealthy and questionable.

Addictions can fall under the category of self-gratifying manifestations of pleasure that fall short of being healthy and sustainable. Being controlled by addictions limits free choice and can set in motion an overindulgence of pleasure-seeking that often leaves you empty. That one more piece of cake, or that "last" pack of cigarettes, or the final affair all fall under the guise of attaining the pleasures from life. The next step is to analyze whether you are truly evoking pleasure or just a temporary pleasurable sensation. Then ask yourself if it's really worth it. Are you willing to lose your mate, risk dying from a disease, put on the extra pounds, or increase your risk of lung and heart disease for a simple fleeting pleasure? You are the only one who can answer these questions because you are the ultimate gauge of what is and is not acceptable, tolerable, or worth it. My main point is to help you see and to understand how easy it is to fall victim to the trap of seeking pleasure.

There is nothing wrong with gravitating to people or situations that make you laugh or make you feel good and add to your state of wellness. This is a very healthy scenario and one not to be confused with the pleasure derived from the experience of some sort of pain. The pleasure of feeling a "high," either from excessive alcohol, mood-altering drugs, or your favorite comfort food is often followed by the pain of a hangover and vomiting; withdrawal and the shakes; or bloating and weight gain. If the price paid is less than the feelings of pleasure you receive, chances are you will continue seeking pleasure via this avenue.

As in the laws of physics and Newton's law of motion, the force required to facilitate a change must be unbalanced to or different from the object or force to elicit movement or change.

A little deeper: Life, as it's being lived, is no longer tolerable or acceptable by you, and your desire to change your life is so great that this can and usually will facilitate a permanent change within your life.

The idea, though, is not to get yourself into a situation where a crisis is created which forces you to make the appropriate changes. If you are convicted of a crime, this forces you to alter your life by the mere fact of imprisonment. You can become sick and hospitalized for a heart attack because you chose to live a sedentary life while eating fast food. The GOOD news is that this is all preventable and controllable by you. You don't have to choose a life with painful pleasure to experience the PLEASURE of life and you don't have to pay a high price for it either. Knowing and understanding your desire to seek pleasure can often assist you in attaining it.

I previously had the tendency to attract men into my life who were aggressive, had a volatile temper, or were abusive on some level. Even though the external appearances and characteristics were very different, the results were the same—some form of unhealthy aggression. I realize my role in the creation of aggression or abuse, NOW, yet in the moment, I felt victimized by it all. I came to realize that (due to childhood trauma), I associated love with abuse and somehow either gravitated to the type of man who had this personality or would unconsciously assist in its facilitation, via argumentativeness. The result was, more often than not, abusive and unhealthy for the both of us.

To reprogram my mind (my computer chip) to the fact that love and abuse are polar opposites and couldn't coexist was not an easy task for me. It took several husbands and multiple relationships to assist me in realizing this fact and in making a proactive choice to STOP this behavior and type of thinking. No matter how much I tried to convince myself that my husband or mate was in love with or loved me, the fact remained that no matter how I tried to calculate the answer, abuse and disrespect did not add up to LOVE. This I had to accept as fact in order for me to change my life and my unhealthy patterns. Love and abuse were SO familiar to me that I didn't know, nor had I learned, how to relate to spouses any differently.

Why do you think it took so long or that I needed so many attempts with relationships for me to "get it"? On one level I can say that it took as long as it needed to take for me to get it. On another level I can say that I either had tunnel vision or was farsighted. Try and imagine an object that is too close within your field of vision (by placing something very close to and in front of your eyes). When you try and focus on it, you usually can only see a blur. This is often what happens within an intimate relationship. You cannot get a clear vision or understanding of what is.

As paintings often require that you step back to fully appreciate and see the detail, so it often is with yourself and your life. It's difficult to see the entire picture of yourself, as you've painted it, until you take a few steps back to view the entire scenario. Often what you felt was SO important only becomes a dot in the whole scheme of things. Distance often gives you a better and more comprehensive perspective of what truly is. If you can give yourself some breathing space to "be" without judging yourself and allow yourself to make adjustments, if needed, then your chances of successfully breaking an unhealthy pattern are significantly increased. The more you are aware of what drives you to choose certain paths, the greater control you have over your creations, and your life.

Let's see what constitutes the self-perpetuation of the pleasure/pain cycle and what would cause a person to remain in a situation that created pain in the first place. It could be an inner need to be punished (a feeling of being a bad person) or the need for excitement and drama (arguments). It could be the need to be right (to prove a theory or belief). Whatever the reason, guaranteed, there is something in it for everyone, or the situation or scenario wouldn't exist. Even abuse, in some fashion, can be a trade-off for what is needed by the recipient, not because that person consciously wants to be harmed, but because he or she may feel that abuse is the price necessarily paid to be in a relationship. Yes, of course, this is most unhealthy, yet is often what drives someone to stay in an unhealthy relationship. I say this because I feel that if you were getting absolutely nothing from a situation or a relationship, you would not be in it. This is not to excuse the abusive behavior. Quite the opposite, it's to acknowledge its existence to allow you to make the appropriate changes.

Let's now travel into the world of self-abuse or self-mutilation for the pleasure of presumed enhanced beauty. Multiple body piercing, tattoos, hair transplants, and plastic surgery, not to mention the wearing of stiletto heels—the list is unending. We are conditioned to believe that there is always something to improve, to beautify, or to extract pleasure from, no matter what price you may have to pay. This mixture of pleasure and pain can be intense, addictive, and in many instances, destructive, leading even to death.

What is the driving force that can lead a seemingly normal person to risk his or her life for the pleasure of seeing and experiencing enhanced beauty? I know I've been there. With my two bouts of plastic surgery (13 and 14 years ago) involving liposuction, mini-abdominoplasty, and a modified thigh tuck, I was aspiring to achieve the ultimate beauty, no matter the price. When I look back and see the risk I put myself through to achieve the "perfect" body, I shiver. I had a much more beautiful body prior to the surgeries. In addition I now carry the scars of the operations that cannot be hidden with makeup or creams. I have constant, daily reminders that I, years ago, disliked and was disconnected from my body SO much that I chose to subject it to being cut so aggressively.

Often when I look at myself in the mirror, I feel such intense sadness for whom I was 14 years ago that it makes me feel like crying. During these times I find myself apologizing to my body for the abuse that I put it through, and all the while it (my body) never failed me. When you can imagine your dearest, closest friend remaining with you and supporting you no matter what you did to her (your body), and always being there for you, it can bring tears to your eyes. If you can imagine that you, with your body, are your deepest and closest friend who loves and supports you no matter what you to do it and never leaves your side, maybe you would think twice about allowing someone to cut into it for the sole purpose of feeling or seeming more beautiful.

What messages are you giving yourself when you say to your body that it needs some form of reconstruction? Even your best friend would feel the pain of rejection. Try not to disassociate yourself from your body. This is the vehicle that has been given to you to travel through life. Beautify it and enhance it from within the wellspring of inner light that you carry and that is inherently yours from birth. Be the beauty that you are and try not to go looking outside yourself for what is already within you.

Let's now look at different scenarios where the intermingling of pleasure and pain would be considered healthy and desirable, such as childbirth. The pain of labor is weighed against the pleasure of giving birth to your child and holding him or her in your arms. You cannot put a value on what was required to give birth. The same holds true for you who invested years of study, discipline, and possible pain and sacrifice to acquire your educational degree. These are good and healthy situations that should not be confused with the former pain/pleasure scenarios.

I strongly feel that unless you can separate and understand the correlation between pleasure and pain, you may make choices that you think will bring you pleasure, when in actuality they can cause you great pain and unpleasantness. This is so important to realize when choosing the directions for your life and what you truly want to manifest. It CAN color the flavor of your manifestations for everything, including health, wealth, a better job, or a loving relationship.

Be gentle with yourself during your self-evaluation, if you choose this route. Allow yourself the space to reflect on the different scenarios that are potential possibilities. Ask yourself if the person, place, or thing that gives you pleasure uplifts you and feeds your soul. Or is the pleasure something transitory and only superficial, on the physical plane? This is a strong clue for you in understanding whether the pleasure you seek has a high price tag or if it comes without strings.

I hope for you to embody fully the understanding that you alone can make yourself happy. You need not have to look over the next hill (outside yourself), to the next tomorrow, to bring yourself the answers you're looking for today. You not only hold the key to your locked doors, you ARE the key and the answer to all your questions.

Become your own best friend and confidante while learning to listen to and trust you. Be conscious of what it is you want from the pleasure, and ask yourself if there is a high price tag required to acquire it. Pain is not the path required to find pleasure and happiness, or for growth and evolution. You can consciously choose joy and pleasure without the pain. You need only decide how you want to travel on your path. Many blessings to you on your journey of self-discovery and may it be truly a rewarding and pleasurable one.

Chapter Twenty-Two

The Sweetness of Life:
Reaching for the Stars

Reach for the Stars

– Twenty-Two –

The Sweetness of Life:
Reaching for the Stars

*E*xperiencing and living the sweetness of life is a normal goal or desire. This desire can drive you to great heights of accomplishment and success. The inner flame of desire and passion is so essential for manifestation that without it, the chances of your realizing your dreams are lessened. The sweet, good life incorporates a life of peace, love, harmony, health, happiness, and wealth in the manner you've chosen. It reflects your conscious awareness, your inner beauty, your inner knowing and connection with your Divinity. It demonstrates your continued growth and evolution, in a timely fashion, with your ability to co-create. It reflects the sweetness, the nectar, of life, of being present. It reflects being in conscious command of your life.

Sweetness of life relates to the joy of being fully alive and REAL. It is not related to the "sugar sweet" of someone who feels the need to be accepted and loved. This is quite the contrary. It relates to the strong and the brave who go out into the world with an open heart, willing to connect to the hearts and souls of others. It relates to the sweetness of love in your heart that radiates warmth. Living the sweet life allows you to manifest from a place of Divinity and power.

In living the sweet life, you would not be controlled by fear or by the feeling that something is lacking. There would be only fullness and abundance. Love, acceptance, and tolerance would be a state of being. Teaching, sharing, and inspiring others would be a way of life. By living the sweet life and living in your heart, you'd be making conscious choices (mental collaboration), loving and taking a stand for yourself (emotional collaboration). You would be gathering knowledge and guidance from your inner Divinity (spiritual collaboration), and taking action in the fulfillment of your goals and heart's desires (physical collaboration). Collaboration and unity of all these facets of life adds to the experience of life's sweetness.

Let's break down these collaborative aspects a little more to demonstrate how they can and do work separately and that in tandem; they operate more strongly and fully. For some reason, both men and women find it hard to keep an open, loving heart in the midst of being strong and authoritative. One avenue is usually chosen over the other and often decisions are made without the support of the whole. When a factor is absent in the decision-making process, something suffers. To choose to fire someone because he or she missed work without permission would be logical under certain circumstances. If you failed to incorporate the appropriate empathetic feelings, if the person missed work, for example, because of the loss of a loved one, you'd be doing a great disservice to that individual and to your ability to make good executive decisions.

When your mind (mental), your heart (emotional), your body (physical), and your divine self (spiritual) are in unison, then and only then can you expect to create from a totally conscious and co-creative position. This in turn will allow you to fulfill your mission here on earth and fully live the "sweet" life.

Envision yourself creating the world you've always dreamed of and the goals you've always wanted to achieve. Envision yourself as the "goddess" that lives within (your Divinity). Utilize the knowledge, power, wisdom, and love to manifest your dreams, goals, and heart's desires. It's the feminine, the goddess within you, who is asking to be awakened and embraced into your life. It's the knowing what you truly are and knowing how much power you hold within. It's the knowing that you hold the key to life as a co-creator with God. It's the knowing that all life originates from the feminine. It's the knowing that you need not prove your strength and power to the world by becoming tough and heartless. It's the knowing that your true power is your feminine. It's the knowing that embodying your feminine is not showing weakness.

It's the knowing that your femininity is your key to manifesting. It's the knowing that you have control over your life and no longer need be a victim of anyone or anything. It's the knowing that you are beautiful just as you are, and your beauty stems from within.

It's the knowing that the more you love, the more love comes back to you. It's the knowing that everyone has his or her own truth and that truth is relative. It's the knowing that truth changes as a person changes. It's the knowing that no one is perfect and the only constant is LOVE. It's the knowing that you have the power. It's the knowing that you have the key to your happiness and to your well-being. It's the knowing that all life needs love, and it's the knowing that you are not alone.

Your wisdom, your understanding of these universal laws, will shine through you, like sparkling diamonds radiating your inner light for all to see. You need not go and proclaim it to the world on the highest mountain. All you need do is interact with others in community, in collaboration, and to connect with their hearts and souls.

You've heard that the eyes are the windows to the soul. I have found this to be true. Connect with the souls of others.

Look into their eyes and see the beauty within. Words need not be spoken when you look into the depths of someone else's eyes. The connection can speak miracles and the bonding can be deep. Much can be conveyed in this manner and it usually is on a higher level of communication. Shine your love from your heart into their hearts and souls and feel the inner connection that is there for all to experience. Know that you are one with all and that there is no separation.

Much is seen and sensed through the eyes, such as regret or happiness. When you let someone into your eyes, you are letting that person into a part of you that is also part of your Divinity, your soul. If you are receptive enough, you will learn to understand and accept others for who they are, a divine being of God. When you relate to others via your open heart and soul, there will be no need to argue or to apologize. Whatever is said with an open heart, whether difficult to hear or not, will be more readily received by others. They will be able to see or sense that your heart and higher intelligence are guiding you.

Choose to interact and communicate with others in a manner that is conducive to happiness, health, and feelings of well-being. Choose to live your life openly, authentically, lovingly, and with purpose. Be the mover and the shaker in your life while making the decisions. Learn to use your God-given talents and gifts, along with others you have mastered, during your stay on this earth. Feel happier and more fulfilled while touching the lives of others. You will make all lives richer and more fulfilling. Make a commitment to yourself and to choose the path of love. Learn to use your tools to manifest what it is you want to create within your life. Know that the more love that permeates from your being, the more love you will be creating and reflecting back to you.

It's literally impossible to be in a state of negativity when in the state of love, so use this fact to arm yourself when in an argument or difficult situation. Know that the Divinity of your love will support you during the difficult scenario and all will realign of its own accord. You need to do nothing other than remain in love because when there is no backboard for the negativity to bounce against, it falls to an eventual stop. Know that in doing so, you are the one who is taking control of yourself and of the situation. You are not being weak or turning the other cheek. You are the one taking action by opening your heart and acting from a loving space. Living this way opens up your world to limitless possibilities and to a life of sweetness and light.

Be happy and loving. Be powerful and strong. Be healthy and wealthy. Be safe and wise. Take a chance. Live your life. Be your feminine. Namaste! Amen!

Summary

*I*n summary, I would like to continue my support with your journey of self-discovery and self-awareness. Please feel free to contact me through my website: www.LivingLifePublishing.com with any questions which you may have. I plan, for the future, to create online classes and chat groups that would continue to offer help and support. I, also, am traveling down this lifelong path of self-discovery and awareness and would hope that together with you, we can make our journeys a little easier and more joyful.

Please feel free to offer your experiences and suggestions, via my website, that you feel would be of benefit to all of us. I plan to have a place to post your comments, suggestions and advice. I feel we each have something unique to offer the other and I hope to create the space for this to occur. Please help assist me with this wonderful possibility, for without your participation this would not exist.

Thank you for this opportunity to come into your home and your life, via my book, and for the unlimited possibilities that can be created from this experience. Let's join forces with each other to help educate and enlighten our world of the power that lies within each of us and of the beautiful and loving qualities that we each possess.

With the greatest respect and warmest regards,

Bianca Guerra

Glossary

Divinity: The godhead, God, Godlike character.

Co-creation: The human and divine act of bringing an artifact into existence.

Conscious Intent: Awareness of aim or purpose.

Inner Guidance: Deep advice or counseling given by your spirit.

Interactive: The capability of acting on or influencing each other.

Manifestation: An indication of the existence, reality, or presence of something. The act of manifesting.

Manipulation: Shrewd or devious management, especially for one's own advantage.

Namaste: A prayer salutation: "The Divine Spirit in me recognizes and honors the Divine Spirit in you". This is usually said while bowing with respect to the other, with the hands held in a prayer position.

Reactive: Tending to be responsive or to react to a stimulus.

Soul: The spiritual nature of humans, regarded as immortal, separable from the body at death, and susceptible to happiness or misery in a future state.

Spirit: The vital principle or animating force within living beings. The Holy Spirit. The part of a human being associated with the mind, will, and feelings.

Index

About the Author

BIANCA GUERRA is a multimedia publisher and producer, socially responsible entrepreneur and philanthropist.

Ms. Guerra is the founder and owner of Bianca Productions LLC, a multimedia production company that develops conscious content for broadcast radio and television, DVD, and broadband Internet distribution. She is also the founder and owner of Living Life Publishing Co., a San Antonio, Texas- and Sausalito, California-based publishing company that develops and publishes books, cards and electronic media dedicated to uplifting and educating its readers.

Ms. Guerra studied energy medicine and the healing arts in Arizona and graduated, in 1993, with honors as a Master Energy Healer. She also studied homeopathy for 2 1/2 years and has applied the knowledge within her personal life. Along with being a self-taught medical intuitive, Ms. Guerra has studied many additional forms of energy and spiritual healing such as Reiki. She was ordained as a hands-on-healing minister in 1992 and earned a Bachelor of Ministerial Science.

She was the founder and owner of Brownsville Physical Therapy and Sports Medicine from 1981 until 1990, when she sold it and moved to Arizona to pursue additional education in holistic and alternative medicine. She learned at an early stage in her career that there was something very significant and healing about her hands, a gift that revealed itself when she touched people. Many of her patients would comment they felt her hands emitting a heat that felt very healing. They often commented that they thought the heat was coming from some form of heat machine. Thus began her quest for additional answers as to why this was happening and what could she do to develop this gift further.

She presently resides in San Antonio, Texas and Sausalito, California and is a member and supporter of the Witte Museum, McNay Museum, Dominion Country Club, Assistance League of San Antonio, the Gardenia Club, and the Ecumenical Consortium. She also donates funds to the Cancer and Heart Associations, and The Unicorn Center.

Ms. Guerra is a member of the American Physical Therapy Association, the National Association of Television Program Executives (NAPTE), a life member and diplomat of The American Association of Integrative Medicine (AAIM), and an advisory board member of The American College of Wellness.

She is also the single mother of two young men, in their mid-20's, who have graduated from universities and of whom she is very proud. At present, her goal is to help educate people about their innate power to heal themselves and their lives and to help others, in this related field, get their message out to the world. She is committed to helping the individual consciously awaken by helping to connect with his or her inner wisdom. She wants to help each individual understand that he or she is powerful and holds the key to his or her own happiness and well-being.

She is a master of manifestation and has proven repeatedly that she, in conjunction with the Divine, is able to create her reality with conscious intent. She is presently in a committed relationship, following 11 years of single life, with her soul mate and has plans on marrying in the near future. Together with her fiancé, she plans to help awaken and educate people on how to become conscious, responsible, and contributing participants in society.

Education

Bianca Guerra was born on January 22, 1952, in Brownsville, Texas. She received a Catholic education from first grade through high school. She attended the local junior College, Texas Southmost College, for one year before transferring to Southwest Texas State University (Texas State University), where she remained for one year. She then transferred to Texas Woman's University, which specialized in her major degree field, and graduated in 1974 with a B.S. degree in Physical Therapy and Biology.

Please visit her websites at:
www.BiancaProductions.com
&
www.LivingLifePublishing.com.

Other Titles by Bianca Guerra

A Woman's Guide to Manifestation
The Inspirational Cards created from her book.
A 44 Card Deck with a 64-page instructional booklet. $15.95
ISBN#: 0-9768773-3-3

A Woman's Guide to Manifestation
The Companion CD created for her book.
An Audio CD with a 32-page booklet. $15.95
ISBN#: 0-9769166-8-1

A Woman's Guide to Manifestation
The Companion DVD created for her book.
A DVD with a 32-page booklet. $24.95
ISBN#: 0-9769166-9-X

InnerScope™
Self-Awareness Cards
A 44 Card Deck with a 40-page instructional booklet. $15.95
ISBN#: 0-9768773-4-1

The 8 Steps to Manifestation
A Handbook to Conscious Creation
A 150-page sequel to the book *A Woman's Guide
to Manifestation Creating Your Reality with
Conscious Intent.* $15.95
ISBN#: 0-9768773-9-2

For more information about the author and/or how to order,
please visit our website at: **www.LivingLifePublishing.com**

Other Titles offered by
Living Life Publishing Co.

SuperLove
By Lou CasaBianca
A beautifully designed and illustrated book
depicting the journey and experience of Sacred Love.

SuperLove Cards
By Lou CasaBianca
A Companion to the book "SuperLove"
A 44 Card Deck with instructional booklet.

SuperLove
By Lou CasaBianca
The Companion CD created for the book.
An Audio CD with a 32-page booklet.

SuperLove
By Lou CasaBianca
The Companion DVD created for the book.
A DVD with a 32-page booklet.

For more information about the author and/or how to order,
please visit our website at:
www.LivingLifePublishing.com

Living Life
Publishing Co.

Purpose and Mission Statement

The purpose of our business, Bianca Productions LLC dba: Living Life Publishing Co., is to help enlighten individuals through education while enriching them with inspirational nourishment, and empowering them through self-awareness of their innate abilities to create their own reality. Bianca Productions LLC and Living Life Publishing Co. incorporate the premise that everyone has the ability to heal themselves and his or her life if only awakened to this inner wisdom.

It is through the medium of radio, television, audio/visuals, and published written materials that this company will focus on helping to bring alternative health, healing, knowledge, abundance and consciousness into the mainstream population.

Mission Statement

"The mission of Living Life Publishing Co. is to help enlighten, enrich and empower the lives of others via the avenue of multimedia. Our goal is to help bring an individual into a heightened sense of awareness of his or her strengths and life's purpose. Living Life Publishing Co. strives to help promote a more socially conscious and responsible person who can help contribute to bringing positive changes into the world."

-Bianca Guerra, October 2004

Quotes from Notable Women in History:

Maya Angelou:

"The honorary duty of a human being is to love."

"Love is that condition in the human spirit so profound that it allows me to survive, and better than that, to thrive with passion, compassion, and style."

Susan B. Anthony:

"Failure is impossible."

"The older I get, the greater power I seem to have to help the world; I am like a snowball — the further I am rolled the more I gain."

Joan Baez:

"To love means you also trust."

"Instead of getting hard ourselves and trying to compete, women should try and give their best qualities to men - bring them softness, teach them how to cry."

Laura Bush:

"The power of a book lies in its power to turn a solitary act into a shared vision. As long as we have books, we are not alone."

Hillary Rodham Clinton:

"There cannot be true democracy unless women's voices are heard."

Indira Gandhi:

"You cannot shake hands with a clenched fist."

"You must learn to be still in the midst of activity and to be vibrantly alive in repose."

Anne Morrow Lindbergh:

"The most exhausting thing in life is being insincere."

"I believe that what a woman resents is not so much giving herself in pieces as giving herself purposelessly."

Golda Meir:

"I never did anything alone. Whatever was accomplished in this country was accomplished collectively."   1977

"At work, you think of the children you've left at home. At home, you think of the work you've left unfinished. Such a struggle is unleashed within yourself, your heart is rent."

Grandma Moses:

"Life is what we make it, always has been, always will be."

Mother Teresa of Calcutta:

"If you judge people, you have no time to love them."

"It is not how much we do, but how much love we put in the doing. It is not how much we give, but how much love we put in the giving."

Florence Nightingale:

"For what is Mysticism? Is it not the attempt to draw near to God, not by rites or ceremonies, but by inward disposition? Is it not merely a hard word for 'The Kingdom of Heaven is within'? Heaven is neither a place nor a time." [1873]

Jacqueline Kennedy Onassis:

"There are many little ways to enlarge your child's world. Love of books is the best of all."

"What is sad for women of my generation is that they weren't supposed to work if they had families."

Margaret Thatcher:

"Any woman who understands the problems of running a home will be nearer to understanding the problems of running a country."

"The woman's mission is not to enhance the masculine spirit, but to express the feminine; hers is not to preserve a man-made world, but to create a human world by the infusion of the feminine element into all of its activities."